THEY WILL RUN

The Golden Age of the Automobile in St. Louis

Reedy Press
PO Box 5131
St. Louis, MO 63139
www.reedypress.com

Cover Design: Barbara Northcott
Book Design: Jill Halpin and Linda Eckels

Library of Congress Control Number: 2019936723

ISBN: 9781681062341

Printed in the United States of America
19 20 21 22 23   5 4 3 2 1

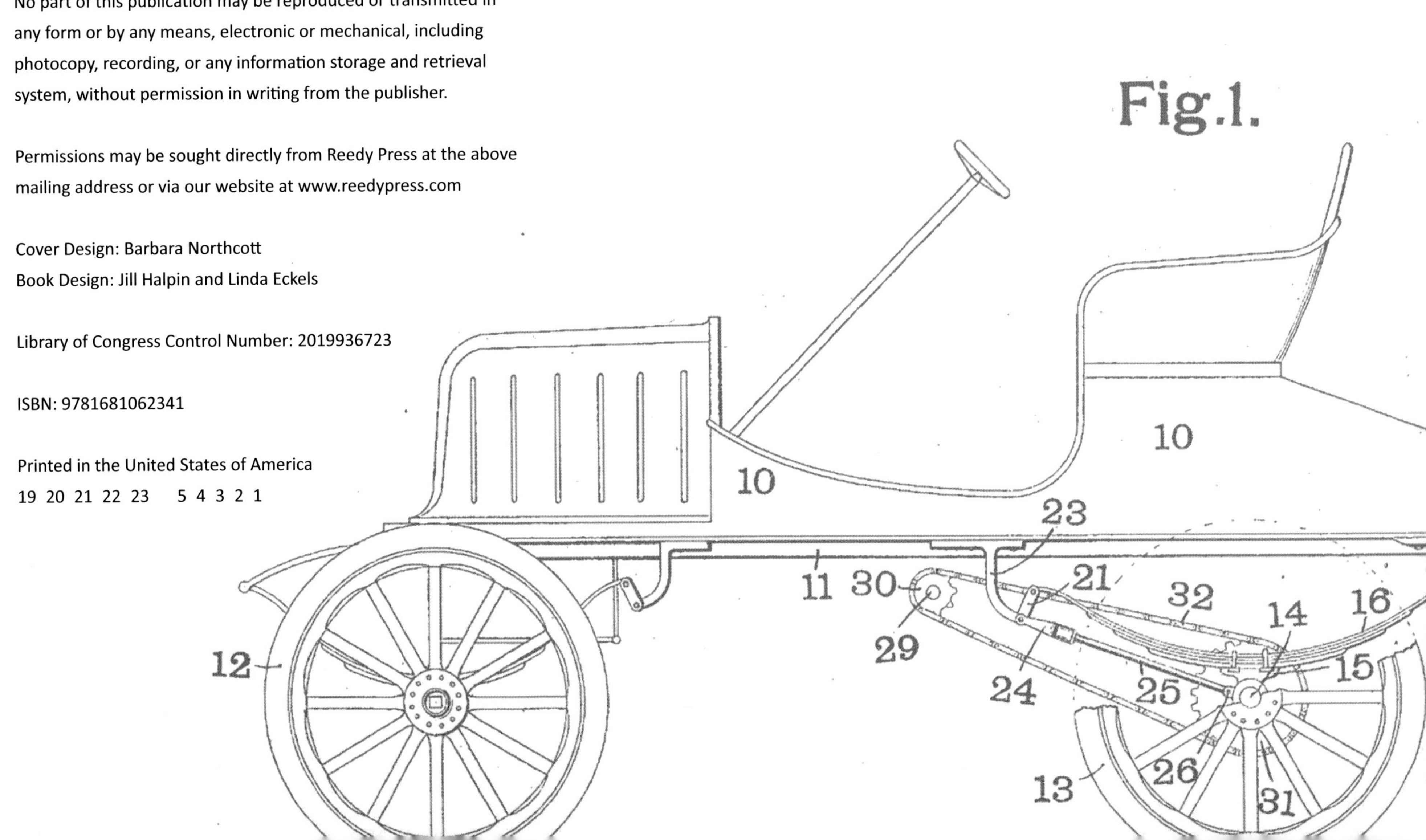

DEDICATION

To Mom and Dad for demonstrating how vehicles you both need and love can open
the world and then encouraging me to write about it.

—Molly (Leugers) Butterworth

To my beloved wife and daughter, who have not only understood but also supported
my passion for automobiles and the loss of their spots in the garage to my vintage wheels.

—Tom Eyssell

A circa 1901 Dyke touring car with what appears to be the Dyke family inside. Courtesy Dorris Family Collection.

THEY WILL RUN

The Golden Age of the Automobile in St. Louis

MOLLY BUTTERWORTH AND THOMAS H. EYSSELL

This Dorris Model IBW two-ton was one of two such chassis the St. Louis Fire Department purchased in April 1918 for a total of $4900. Master Mechanic Chris Koeln oversaw the building of both as hose and chemical cars. Both were rebuilt in 1930 and remained in service until 1943. Courtesy Greg R. Rhomberg, the Antique Warehouse.

Table of Contents

Dorris built buses for both commuter and cross-country lines. Courtesy Dorris Family Collection.

FOREWORD

There is no one alive who remembers a world without automobiles. I knew my grandfather as a nice, happy old guy who didn't have much to do with children like me. Others remember him for his achievements as an automobile pioneer. Perhaps it's our custom to remember a person by their work rather than by who they were as a person, but it seems that being a nice person doesn't get much attention these days.

My grandfather was born in 1874 and was two years old when Custer lost his life at the Little Bighorn. The eastern and western sections of this country's first transcontinental railroad had met in Utah just five years before. The only way to leave the country was by boat or walking. Personal freedom was exercised by exercising, riding a horse or with a horse drawn wagon, walking or by catching a streetcar at the corner. Trains worked. The automobile changed the way we live and changed our planet in ways neither my grandfather's generation nor subsequent ones have yet come to grips with.

As the elevator changed the way buildings and cities look, the auto changed our streets, houses and cities as well as our how we spend our time and money. Has anyone ever questioned why things are the way they are? Who connected our view of our own ego with what kind of car we drive? Why do we care so much about an appliance?

The modern automobile has been perfected to the point that it is no longer doubtful it will start and get us to where we want to go. Today's automobiles have no more personality than the refrigerator.

As someone who has owned several cars that had so much personality that I hated owning them, perhaps one that works as expected is a blessing. But it ain't a part of the family.

Our family has always named our cars. My grandfather's experimental auto was named "Rosie." She started life in 1919 as a bright red touring car, the Dorris Motor Car Company's experimental vehicle, also used as the Chief Engineer and Designer's family car. If it didn't work (and as with any experiment, sometimes they don't), he took the streetcar. Rosie is still in the family. She is recovering from a trip my grandfather took with two of his brothers toward California in 1954. The car was okay; she had an engine he modified with an overhead cam, but the driver had to be hospitalized before they got to where they were going. They had a grand time! Oh, the stories!

The automobile used to connect us with friends we just hadn't met yet. They were open to the world. People could see who was driving and the folks in the car could make contact with people on the street. There was nothing else to do, in the beginning, as radio, cell phones, tinted windows, and air conditioning had not yet isolated the driver from the world. If we can't see who is driving, how does that help your ego?

My father told me that his father selected St. Louis as the place to build automobiles because the train fare from his home in Nashville, Tennessee, to our lovely town was about a dollar cheaper than that to Detroit. In the late 1890s St. Louis was THE place to be. Still is.

—Andy Dorris

The Polar Wave Ice and Fuel Company, until the 1950s the largest ice and fuel company in St. Louis, believed in the quality of Dorris trucks. Courtesy Dorris Family Collection.

"My mom used to work on the Explorer engine line at the Ford plant . . . "

"I can't believe every vehicle in this car show was built here in St. Louis before the war!"

"Corvettes used to be built right there?"

A driver, occupant, or fan of the modern automobile need not travel far in reverse gear to open a map of the myriad sites in St. Louis that once played or still play a role in the design, manufacture, and sale of the vehicles that have become the primary mode of transportation in the United States. But finding the right roads on that map can require a little research and planning before the trip, as, in some cases, well over a century has passed since that was built here or they invented that over there.

In the following pages are the stories of the people who recognized the advantages St. Louis has provided innovators and builders for centuries, who embraced and improved the horseless carriage, and whose work helped expand the city's definition as a transportation hub. The contributions it made and continues to make to the vehicles we drive are so significant that the car or truck in your driveway, garage, or parking spot has very few degrees of separation from something invented, created, and built in the Gateway City.

For almost a century, the automobile manufacturing industry was characterized by large capital requirements, small but steady improvements in technology, safety, and mileage, and the dominance of a relatively small number of large players.

Today the automobile industry is at a crossroads. Long-time manufacturers are being disrupted by new technologies and players (think autonomous vehicles, Apple, and Google), by new (or revived) fuels—the long dominance of the gasoline engine appears to be nearing its end. While electric- and steam-powered vehicles vied for supremacy with the internal combustion engine at the turn of the twentieth century, gasoline power quickly won the battle as a result of its convenience, its "bang for the buck" (in terms of the energy stored in relatively small amounts of fuel), and because of the cruising range it provided. For decades, the old joke was, "The electric vehicle is the car of the future—and always will be."

However, rapidly improving battery technology, as well as materials and software advances have resulted in a rash of both hybrids and electric vehicles (EVs) hitting the market. Virtually all of the major manufacturers now offer EVs, and a number of smaller ones are jumping into the market along with them. And hydrogen-powered automobiles—which produce zero emissions—have already been offered by Honda, Toyota, and Hyundai.

In light of these developments, it's worthwhile to stop and take a look backward: how did we get here, and, more importantly, what role did St. Louis play in the development of the automobile

WINDSOR

RUXTON

Moon
MOTOR CAR CO.
– 1906 –

The
CAR DELUXE

1925

Ford
MODEL T

HERCULES

1920

CRESCENT

1905

A.B.C.

Motor Vehicle Co.
ST. LOUIS, MISSOURI

industry? We have created this book to answer exactly these questions and to bring to light some of the key St. Louis people and organizations who were involved.

If you're holding this book, you are probably interested in St. Louis history. And St. Louis has a proud history stretching back over 250 years. Most everyone knows St. Louis was once described as "first in brews, first in shoes," and that Lewis and Clark started their famous trek from St. Louis.

But how many people know that St. Louis was home to some of the earliest creators of the automobile? Or that St. Louis was at one point second only to Detroit in the manufacture of American automobiles? That St. Louis was the home of the first gasoline station dedicated to serving motorists? Or that St. Louis was the home of the first automobile parts supply house?

The list goes on and on. And in the next several chapters, you will learn about these firsts and many more—you will meet dreamers, builders, businessmen, aesthetes, butchers, and brewers. In short, you will meet a cast of characters that one couldn't dream up: the auto men.

We hope that you enjoy reading this book as much as we enjoyed writing it. And we hope that you will come away with an even greater appreciation of all things St. Louis—a "gateway city" in so many ways!

Sincerely,
Molly Butterworth and Thomas Eyssell

Although the vehicle department of Anheuser-Busch boasted being among the first to design and build refrigerated trucks, Dorris was alongside them with their own system. Courtesy Dorris Family Collection.

A bigger Dorris 6-80 seven passenger featuring a 132-inch wheelbase, photographed in front of the World's Fair Pavilion in Forest Park circa 1920. Courtesy Dorris Family Collection.

When Josh Stevens of Reedy Press asked Steve Tiemann, a colleague of one of the authors and the photographer for one of Reedy's many works related to the history of St. Louis, if he knew of anyone who might write a book covering the long and significant automotive heritage of the Gateway City, Steve mentioned his colleague's name. We thank both Steve and Josh for giving us the keys to this car.

We also extend our gratitude to Greg R. Rhomberg of the Antique Warehouse, Mary Zettwoch of the University of Missouri–St. Louis Library and Charles Brown of the University of Missouri–St. Louis Mercantile Library, Lauren Sallwasser of the Missouri Historical Society, the State Historical Society of Missouri, the Detroit Public Library, Jim Livingston, the Antique Automobile Club of America, the Horseless Carriage Club of Missouri, Cartype, the *St. Louis Post-Dispatch*, Shorpy, the Landmarks Association of St. Louis, the Western Antique Aeroplane and Automobile Museum, the Penngrove Power and Implement Museum, the University City Public Library, Robert Gardner, the Museum of American Speed, Getty Images, the Missouri State Archives, Next St. Louis, the US Army and World War II Database, the Library of Congress, the Associated Press, the World War II Database, General Motors, the National Corvette Museum, Dean's Garage, Jim and Chester's Garage, Clark Properties, Gray Design Group, Wiegmann Associates, Chrysler Motors, LoopNet, Rivian, the Danforth Center, Jesse Francis of Faust County Park, Chuck Leugers, Greg Fox, and the residents of, business owners along, and US Postal Service employees carrying mail on St. Louis's three Automobile Rows for sharing their buildings, time, knowledge, and, in a few cases, their parking spots.

J. C. Wild created and hand-colored this lithograph of the St. Louis levee and
Front Street circa 1840. The steamer *Alton* is shown at the head of a long
line of riverboats moored at the levee. Near the *Alton*, two Native Americans
appear to be contemplating the profusion of activity on the levee. Courtesy
Missouri History Museum, St. Louis.

Chapter One
LAYING THE BRICKS

While "location, location, location" might be a catchphrase of the twentieth century, the importance of proximity to certain natural features predates real estate signs and open houses by several centuries. Over a thousand years before the St. Louis Cardinals won their first World Series in major league baseball, the land around their Sportsman's Park in St. Louis, Missouri, appealed to Native Americans of the early Mississippian tribes because of the large rivers that bordered it to the east and north. The quality of the soil would support the maize crops that would feed the native settlers, and, nearly as important, the rivers would allow the trade commerce of the tribes to flourish. The most visible indications of their settlements are the earthen mounds they built, primarily as support structures and burial sites. The Cahokia mound, eight miles east of the future site of St. Louis, was the largest city north of Mexico by 1050 CE, and on the ground that would become downtown St. Louis, at least twenty-seven mounds were built. The Mississippians also recognized the appeal of the ground that would later become Forest Park; at least fourteen mounds there were levelled to construct the 1904 World's Fair.

Big Mound, Fifth and Mound Streets, Thomas Easterly,
1852. Courtesy Missouri History Museum, St. Louis.

European settlers took to the rivers in their own explorations. Canadians Louis Jolliet and Father Jacques Marquette left what is now Michigan in 1763, hoping to head south, find the Mississippi River, and travel it to the Pacific Ocean. Before realizing the river headed south rather than west and turning around, Jolliet and Marquette found the confluence of the Mississippi and Missouri rivers and recognized the value of the St. Louis area. One year later, Pierre Laclède Liguest and stepson Auguste Chouteau created a trading post at the site, and construction of wood and brick buildings began near the river.

While President Thomas Jefferson's acquisition from France of 827,000 square miles of land between the Mississippi River and the Rocky Mountains for fifteen million dollars in 1803 was one of the most significant and valuable achievements of the young United States, it was also a risky purchase given how little the Europeans knew

The founding of St. Louis, 1764. Chromolithograph by National Colortype Co. after painting by E. Cameron, 1902. Supplement to the *St. Louis Globe-Democrat*, Feb. 28, 1902. Missouri History Museum, St. Louis Photographs and Prints Collections. Courtesy Missouri History Museum, St. Louis.

Photographer William G. Swekosky caught the three modes of transportation that shaped St. Louis—river, road, and rail—in this image of the St. Louis Harbor Office taken in the late 1940s or early 1950s. The plaque reads, "Here Landed on September 23, 1806 the Lewis and Clark Expedition that disclosed to the world an unknown empire." The ruler near the entrance measured high water marks in the history of St. Louis, and a billboard near the Mississippi River reads, "Ford worth more when you buy!" Courtesy Missouri History Museum, St. Louis.

about the land. Recognizing the value of St. Louis as a launching point given its location on major rivers and the supplies available in it, Army officers Meriwether Lewis and William Clark chose the city as the start of their expedition in 1804 to fulfill President Jefferson's request to travel and document the land included in the purchase.

The success of their journey and return to St. Louis further elevated the profile of the young city and established its role as the gateway to the newly available west. Helping settlers travel through that gate was an opportunity St. Louisans embraced and developed.

1817

Technological innovation helped that gate swing a little more quickly when the first steam-powered boat, the *Zebulon Pike*, reached St. Louis on August 2, 1817. Though the single sidewheeler steamboat presented distance and speed unknown to those who had only experienced paddling and wind as marine power, it did not make things easy for its crew. The boat was the second-smallest steamboat documented on the Mississippi River, and its steam power was very weak and unable to battle currents. The men assigned to the steamer needed a full month and sometimes poles to help push the boat along in its travel from Louisville, Kentucky, to St. Louis.

The levee or Landing, St. Louis, Missouri, 1857, as featured in Ballou's *Pictorial Drawing Room Companion*. Courtesy Missouri History Museum, St. Louis.

1840

The timeless American yearning for more vehicle power propelled further development of the steam boiler and its application in river boats. By the 1840s, steamboats had the size and power to carry European settlers and their belongings on the Missouri River as a primary leg in their journeys to homestead in the American West. The unequaled location of St. Louis made the city a key player in the westward expansion of the United States, and its entrepreneurial businessmen had over six hundred steamboats and four hundred wholesale houses operating at the city's Mississippi River levee by 1849.

The *Zebulon Pike*. *A Pictorial History of St. Louis*. Courtesy Missouri History Museum, St. Louis.

The St. Louis Levee, as photographed by Thomas Easterly in 1853. Courtesy Missouri History Museum, St. Louis.

The first locomotive for the new Pacific Railroad is delivered by boat to the St. Louis levee, 1852. Courtesy Missouri State Archives.

A newspaper ad for the Pacific Railroad in 1859. Courtesy Missouri History Museum, St. Louis.

PACIFIC RAILROAD.

The most Reliable and Direct Route for
KANSAS CITY, LEAVENWORTH & ST. JOSEPH.
Trains Leave St. Louis as follows:
MAIL TRAIN—Daily, at 9:00 A. M., stopping at all Stations and running through to Syracuse.
EXPRESS TRAIN—Daily (except Sunday) at 3:50 P. M., stopping at principal stations, and running to Jefferson City only.
FRANKLIN ACCOMMODATION—Every day (except Sunday) at 5¼ P. M.
Through to Jefferson City in SIX HOURS.
The trains of this road connect at Jefferson City with a daily line of first class
PASSENGER PACKETS,
Which leave immediately on arrival of Express Train for all points on the Missouri River, connecting at Kansas City and Leavenworth with daily lines of stages for Fort Riley and the interior.
Passengers taking this line will avoid detention at St. Louis, save 50 miles in distance, and escape the delays of 155 miles of difficult river navigation, and make the trip from
ST. LOUIS to KANSAS CITY in 48 Hours!
From Syracuse, stages leave daily at 7:30 P. M., (on arrival of mail train from St. Louis), for Springfield (South-West Missouri), Independence (through Georgetown and Warrensburg), and on every Monday and Thursday P. M. the Overland mail Stages of Butterfield & Co.
Through to San Francisco in twenty-three days!
Fare as Low as by any other Route.
Passengers arriving on Eastern and Northern (Morning) trains, have plenty of time to connect with the Express Train of this road.
Passengers arriving at Jefferson City, pass directly aboard the packets, and proceed on their route without incurring extra expense.
Baggage checked to its destination, and transferred to boat free of charge.
Through Tickets may be obtained, securing meals and berths on boat, at the Passenger Depot, corner of Seventh and Poplar streets, or at the Company's Through Ticket Office, No. 42 Fourth street, under the Planters' House; also, at all the principal Railroad Offices in the United States and Canadas.
**E. W. WALLACE, Gen. Ticket Agent.
T. McKISSOCK, Superintendent.**

St. Louisans recognized the necessity of railroads to keep their city competitive. Eleven of those businessmen met in the office of the St. Louis Insurance Company on January 31, 1850, to incorporate the Pacific Railroad with the obvious goal of building a railroad to tie St. Louis to the Pacific Ocean. The new railroad lured engineer James P. Kirkwood away from the Erie Railroad to survey, create routes for, and manage the construction of the tracks, including the first man-made tunnels west of the Mississippi River. The Pacific Railroad carried its first passenger train on December 9, 1852.

But by then, two things were already working against St. Louis in the transportation arena: its delay in developing railroads and, ironically, the Mississippi River. When Chicago passed St. Louis in transportation business during the American Civil War, a group of St. Louis bankers and business owners decided to take on the challenge of crossing the river by rail and created the St. Louis Bridge and Iron Company. In 1867, the new company hired self-trained engineer James Buchanan Eads to not only design but also manage the construction of a bridge across the Mississippi River. The brilliant Eads engineered a double-deck bridge to carry both rail and horse-drawn traffic and implemented pneumatic caissons, tubular cord members, a cantilevered superstructure, and steel rather than cast iron in the design—all innovations in bridge construction. Eads's bridge was also the first in the world engineered and built to carry heavy railroad equipment, and it remarkably used what, at the time, were the longest arch spans in the world. The Eads Bridge, built at a cost of ten million dollars, opened in 1874 and also opened St. Louis to the states and railroads to its east.

Yet as they watched the companies along the levee flourish, St. Louis business owners perceived a challenge from Chicago. The city to the north began to compete with the Gateway City's position as the transportation hub of the midwestern United States, offering something that St. Louis didn't have: railroads. The first railroad to serve Chicago was chartered in 1836, and when it started laying its first tracks in 1848, some

Early construction of the Eads Bridge, September 1873. Courtesy Missouri History Museum, St. Louis.

An entrance to the Eads Bridge on the St. Louis side was torn down in 1888. Courtesy Missouri History Museum, St. Louis.

The completed Eads Bridge seen from the Illinois side of the Mississippi River, 1874. Courtesy Missouri History Museum, St. Louis.

The wheels able to cross the Mississippi River brought inventions to St. Louis from Europe and the eastern United States, including an innovation in human-powered wheels. The safety bicycle, invented in Europe and introduced to the United States by the Overman Wheel Company in Massachusetts in 1882, made simpler, safer, and cheaper bicycles incredibly appealing throughout the country and particularly in larger cities like St. Louis. Recognizing not only the potential popularity of bicycles but also the need for rideable, paved roads, the League of American Wheelmen was created in Newport, Rhode Island, in 1880. It quickly became not only the most popular cyclists' organization in the country but also the country's primary promoter of improved roads. The club's bicyclists were joined by farmers and businesses in seeking paved roads for safety and efficiency as well as reduced costs for transporting goods, and the club created the "Good Roads Movement" and a supporting periodical in 1892. St. Louis, in which a cycling club had been established in 1887 and over 45 miles of granite-covered roads had been built, was recognized by the League as the city with the best roads in 1894.

1882

Members of the League of American Wheelmen posed at the Frank Blair statue in the northeast corner of Forest Park before their second annual St. Louis County Bicycle Tour in 1894. Courtesy Missouri History Museum, St. Louis.

The headquarters of the National Good Roads Association at 408 Olive photographed in 1903 by George Stock. Courtesy Missouri History Museum, St. Louis.

The Packard exhibit at the 1904 World's Fair. Courtesy Missouri History Museum, St. Louis.

Electric automobiles operated by World's Fair Auto Transportation Company offered four-mile-long tours of the 1904 World's Fair with the chauffeurs acting as tour guides. Courtesy Missouri History Museum, St. Louis.

Word of another wheeled innovation, this time the horseless carriage, reached St. Louis at the perfect time for it to dovetail with the popularity of bicycling and further inspire residents of the transportation-minded city to improve its roads. Colonel William H. Moore, predicting the massive impact of the horseless carriage, created the National Good Roads Organization in St. Louis in 1891.

The new group opened offices in the Laclede Building at 408 Olive Street and later moved to 3230 Locust Street.

The group seized upon the opportunities afforded by St. Louis hosting the Louisiana Purchase Exposition, more commonly known as the 1904 World's Fair, by holding the National and International Good Roads Convention on April 27–29, 1904, just

The offices of the Automobile Club of St. Louis, as photographed in 1921 by W. C. Persons. Courtesy Missouri History Museum, St. Louis.

days before the fair opened. The invitation to the convention stated that "the chief subject demanding public attention" was "industrial improvements; the most important of which is 'The Betterment of the Common Roads.'"[1] Over two thousand delegates attended, and President Theodore Roosevelt stated in an opening speech at the convention, "we should have a right to demand that such a nation should build good roads."[2] Colonel Moore also created "Good Roads Trains," which carried donated road building equipment throughout several states to demonstrate to spectators, particularly farmers, the need to build improved roads to carry passengers and goods.

The proverbial squeaky wheel continued to be greased by membership organizations. The Automobile Club of St. Louis was formed in 1902, initially to continue the good roads movement and then to create laws for the new motorized vehicles. It helped write the state of Missouri's first such laws in 1907; these laws included the establishment of speed limits as well as a road improvement fund supported by vehicle licensing fees. The club became the Automobile Association of Missouri in 1921 and was an early participant in the American Automobile Association.

The ability of both the automobile and the train to more adequately fulfill the need for speed pulled passengers and goods off boats and put them on roads and rails. By World War I, the St. Louis levee and the city's entire Mississippi riverfront were much quieter than they had been a half-century earlier. The construction of elevated railroad tracks along the levee was a very visible example of railroads pulling traffic from the rivers. In 1934, more than forty-six thousand phony ballots ensured that a rigged bond measure, ostensibly to create a riverfront memorial to Thomas Jefferson and his goal of westward expansion, passed. In reality, as admitted by then city engineer W. C. Bernard, the real objective was to use federal money in "an enforced slum clearance program." The city proceeded with the demolition of forty square blocks of brick buildings near the river; those buildings

had housed 240 businesses and over five thousand employees. The Terminal Railroad trestle remained until 1961, when the railroads it served finally determined to pay the cost of building tunnels to carry rail traffic from the busy Twelfth Street and Tucker Avenue yards to the northbound mainlines.

The city's quiet, partial "goodbye" to the Mississippi and Missouri rivers went largely unnoticed. St. Louisans' attention was now focused on the new roads carrying vehicles and more particularly the vehicles themselves—many of which were being built right at home in St. Louis.

The St. Louis levee in 1928. Courtesy Missouri History Museum, St. Louis.

This illustrated postcard showing the Automobile Club of Missouri's general office building at 3917 Lindell Boulevard dates to the 1930s. Courtesy Missouri History Museum, St. Louis.

1 SHSMO, National Good Roads Association Papers, 1903-04.
2 Val Hart, *The Story of American Roads* (New York: William Sloane Associates, Inc., 1950) p. 174.

Mr. and Mrs. J. F. Kraft in a steam buggy built by Kraft, circa 1901. Courtesy Missouri History Museum, St. Louis.

CLOSING THE BARN
AND OPENING THE GARAGE

St. Louisans of the nineteenth century had already been conditioned to not only find but also cultivate methods of powered transportation in their young city, given the role their rivers played in helping European emigrants explore and settle the western United States. Watching how steam power had transformed both water and later—through railroads—land travel, residents of what was one of the young country's finest bicycling towns discovered quickly how the new horseless carriages invented in Germany could revolutionize the use of not only St. Louis's miles of improved roads but also the roads and trails created for riders and drivers of horses. They did not rest on their laurels, waiting for others to jump in the new industry, but instead began inventing, building, and selling.

1890

Electric currents were the current thought for starting and powering automobiles in the city in the 1890s. Herbert Wagner and Ferdinand Schwedtmann, inspired by not only the need of the newfangled electric streetcar for dynamos and transformers but also the prediction that the new horseless carriages would require electric starters, started Wagner Electric at 2017 Lucas Place, later Locust Street, in downtown St. Louis in 1891. Just two years later, after seeing horseless carriages while studying abroad in Paris, J. D. Perry Lewis finished building his battery-powered, chain-driven, tiller-steered horseless carriage—the very first in St. Louis. Its top speed of eight miles per hour was more than double the speed of a horse-drawn buggy, and he coincidentally was traveling in the 3000 block of Locust—later a hub of automotive manufacturing and sales in St. Louis—when the rear axle of his vehicle broke and stranded him.

Patent lawyer and mechanical engineer John C. Higdon, working from the Missouri Trust Building in downtown St. Louis, jumped into the automotive industry and chose a single-cylinder gasoline motor to power a simple buggy body for his first car. As no gas combustion engines were being built in St. Louis at the time, Higdon had the car built in Kansas City. Designed to run as an advertising wagon, the vehicle successfully traveled throughout Missouri, Kansas, and Nebraska in the summer and fall of 1896. Excited and eager to share his vehicle's success, Higdon initially made drawings for his vehicle available at no charge to other builders. He argued in the November 21, 1900, issue of the periodical *Horseless Age* that the 1895 Selden patent for using gasoline compression engines and friction clutches in road vehicles should have never been granted, not only because the Selden design did not use a required flywheel but because it lacked mechanical innovation that differed from steam and electric power. However, after building vehicles commercially for his Success Auto Buggy Manufacturing Company (later Success Automobile Manufacturing Company) beginning in 1905, lawyer Higdon wished he had obtained his own patents on aspects of his vehicles.

Seeing the impact of steam power within the maritime and railroading industries convinced J. F. Kraft to use water rather than batteries or gasoline for his steam car of 1896. His buggy with bicycle tires featured a coal-burning boiler behind the driver's seat and was designed to look like the city's horse-drawn steam-powered fire engine.

A similarly unrestrained approach to mechanized road travel was undertaken by Daniel Piskorski, who built a "bicycle aeroplane" in the basement of his residence at 1229 North Tenth Street. After

H. F. Borbein and Company parts catalog, issued 1904.

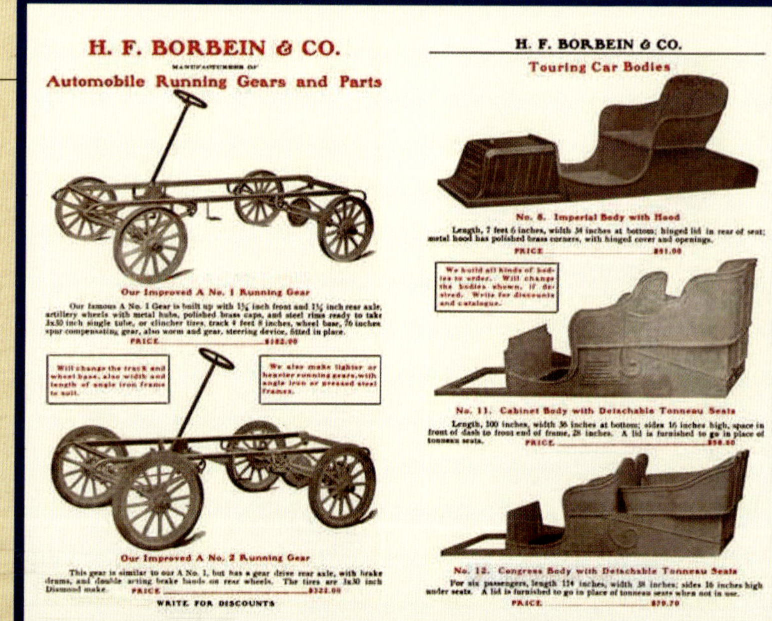

The Auto Repair Company, located on Olive Street west of Vandeventer, was operated by Charles A. Marien and photographed for this image in 1902. It is often recognized as one of the first auto repair shops in St. Louis. Courtesy Missouri History Museum, St. Louis.

St. Louis Gas Engine Company to provide a gasoline motor for him to use in what would become the first gasoline-powered horseless carriage built in St. Louis, completed in 1898. The "Stanhope" body provided by Borbein quickly became popular among local builders, and overall business boomed sufficiently to require a larger manufacturing building by the turn of 1900. Borbein then acquired 1113 Cass Avenue in immediate north St. Louis.

The Borbein Auto Company's assembly plant was hard at work in this 1907 photograph. Courtesy Missouri History Museum, St. Louis.

completing the vehicle, he dismantled it, moved it upstairs and outside, and tested it for curious onlookers.

After observing St. Louisans' growing interest in building horseless carriages, Henry F. Borbein decided to open a small factory in 1898 that built running gear, chassis, bodies, and other parts at the corner of Ninth Street and Clark Avenue. While many early builders favored using traditional wire wheels on multi-section axles, H. F. Borbein and Company was committed to using artillery wood wheels on solid steel axles—advances that would help facilitate the move from chain-driven axles to differential rear axles with drive shafts. Borbein then called upon friends and business neighbors Louis Langan and C. E. Brooks of the

The same year Borbein began manufacturing parts, Andrew Lee Dyke, a native of Dykesville, Louisiana, built an electric runabout in St. Louis for his newly formed St. Louis Electric Automobile Company. One year later, in 1899, he created the St. Louis Automobile and Supply Company—the very first automobile supply firm in the United States—and opened his shop on Locust Street in what would later become Automobile Row. His company not only sold runabout, touring car, and

George Preston Dorris, having successfully built a test car in 1897 that utilized a variant of the 196-cubic-inch marine four-cycle, twin-cylinder engine he had designed to replace the steam power in his Cumberland River excursion boat, convinced childhood friend John French to begin a horseless carriage-building company in St. Louis. The first automotive manufacturing company in the Gateway City, the St. Louis Motor Carriage Company, was opened by the young men thanks in large part to five thousand dollars in stock purchased by French's mother. In 1899, the company delivered just two cars, copies of Dorris's 1897 car now serving as the shop truck. In 1900, production was up from two to thirty. But in 1901, Dorris introduced and began building the clutch and transmission en bloc with the engine. This patented unit powerplant was not only the first application of that engineering and manufacturing technology but also a signature of the St. Louis Motor Carriage vehicles. An extension of the engine's crankcase housed the clutch and sliding gear transmission, allowing oil to flow freely between the two. The thickness of the housing kept the bearings and shaft aligned, and that extension housing allowed operators to easily check the gear conditioning and oil levels. The invention did not provide increased speed but, perhaps more importantly, provided incredible durability, allowing Dorris and French to honestly use the marketing slogan "Rigs That Run."

Though the death of John French is often attributed to being hit by a streetcar in Pittsburgh in 1903 while delivering a St. Louis Motor Car to its new owner, Dorris family members believe he actually survived the accident and returned to St. Louis. They believe he then married his fiancée and, while on a trip with her that same year, became ill, never recovered, and died. His family then moved the St. Louis Motor Carriage Company to Peoria, Illinois. However, Dorris stayed in St. Louis and formed a company that would become one of St. Louis's "Big Three" automobile builders.

The original St. Louis Motor Carriage factory building at 1211–13 North Vandeventer, 1899. Courtesy Missouri History Museum, St. Louis.

delivery wagon bodies, but also sold gasoline engines and all the parts needed to build an automobile. Dyke called the complete kits minus the engine "outfits," and home mechanics sometimes utilized their own steam engines in the Dyke bodies. At least two such examples of the steamers survive today. Dyke also created the first home-study courses for mechanics and began writing automotive service manuals, and after he sold the renamed A. L. Dyke Automobile Supply Company to partners Robert and Roy Britton, Dyke devoted his time to writing. He continued to write *Dyke's Automobile and Gasoline Engine Encyclopedia* for over a half-century.

Dyke initially had the parts for his retail business manufactured in the shop of a man who would become one of his lifelong friends. Nashville native and former Vanderbilt Engineering School student

ST. LOUIS'S DYMANIC DUO
GEORGE DORRIS AND A. L. DYKE

St. Louis automobile history would look very different but for the friendship of George Dorris and A. L. Dyke. Dyke's interest in automobiles was sparked when he watched Dorris working on an early vehicle in the 1890s. Dyke and Dorris remained lifelong friends and embarked on a driving tour in a 1902 St. Louis in 1948.

© Arteaga Studio, courtesy Missouri History Museum, St. Louis.

Owners of St. Louis Motor Carriage Company, George Dorris (front) and Jesse French Jr., John's brother, and Sr., John's father, in a company racing and touring car built in 1902 or 1903 in front of Frank P. Blair Statue at northeast corner of Forest Park on Lindell, circa 1903. Courtesy Missouri History Museum, St. Louis.

Top: St. Louis Motor Carriage workers assembling transmissions in 1902. Courtesy Missouri History Museum, St. Louis. Bottom left: Jesse French Sr. at the wheel of a 1904 St. Louis built at the St. Louis Motor Carriage Company. Courtesy Missouri History Museum, St. Louis. Bottom right: George P. Dorris at the wheel of the St. Louis Motor carriage company sixteen-horsepower touring car that won the ten-mile "Free for All" races during the 1902 St. Louis fair. Courtesy Missouri History Museum, St. Louis. Inset: Even Detroit's public library knows an original St. Louis Motor Cars promotional brochure is worthy of preservation. Courtesy Detroit Public Library.

As the popularity of not only home-built but also factory-built horseless carriages grew in St. Louis, so too did the need to service and fuel those vehicles. German wagon builder Louis Niebling settled in St. Louis in in 1887 and began building wagons and coaches at 1707 South Broadway in 1892. When the 1895 tornado took his building, Niebling built a larger two-story building at 2416 South Twelfth with the idea of beginning to build bodies for and service automobiles, which he began doing in 1899. By 1905, the company was building Mack truck bodies.

Oscar Lawrence Halsey saw an opportunity to generate revenue by selling automobiles made outside St. Louis and began to prepare the city's first car dealership at 3908–18 Olive Street in late 1899. By early 1900, the Halsey Automobile Company introduced Packards to St. Louis. Within a couple of years, after adding Wintons, Franklins, and Cadillacs to its sales inventory, it further expanded its Olive Street dealership. A decade later, it would move to Automobile Row on Locust Street.

George Dorris and his sister in a 1901 St. Louis. Courtesy Missouri History Museum, St. Louis.

As with many "firsts," the question of who built the city's first automobile dealership is open to discussion. Henry Smith "Harry" Turner III suggests that he brought the first automobile to St. Louis (a difficult claim to prove!) and opened the first automobile agency (almost equally difficult to prove!).

"Having learned so much that I now know nothing, I shall proceed to write a book." So begins *Autobiography of a Failure* by Harry Turner, who may qualify as one of St. Louis's most unusual characters of the early twentieth century. A descendant of one of the city's leading families, Harry was a member of high society until he was unceremoniously dropped from the social register for writing a mildly scandalous "tell-all" about some of its members. He was a bon vivant who favored free love, married a dancer, and was convicted of obscenity for an article that appeared in *Much Ado*, a highly regarded literary magazine he published with his wife, Alice.

Harry and Alice moved to the Mississippi riverfront's "Little Bohemia" following the obscenity trial, and it was there that he died a few years later at the relatively young age of fifty-seven. His death remains controversial to this day: Harry drowned after jumping into the Mississippi River at Christmastime. His body later washed ashore with a gash on the head. It remains unknown whether he intended to take a December swim or to commit suicide.

Turner's story intersected with St. Louis automobile history when, in 1899, he purchased a Stanley Steamer and brought it to St. Louis. In his *Autobiography of a Failure*, Turner writes that his Stanley Steamer "was the first automobile the people of St. Louis or I had ever seen, and naturally it attracted much attention on the streets."

As a result of this attention, Turner started one of the first automobile agencies in St. Louis, which quickly became successful. However, Turner's feelings about the horseless carriage seem to reflect his generally bemused outlook on life. He wrote:

"It led finally to my taking an agency for the manufacturer and opening a small store. I wanted something to do, and this did not seem to be a legitimate business. It was perfectly marvelous how those things sold. Sober, solid business men would journey up to my little store on Twelfth Street and pay seven or eight hundred dollars for a toy that was not only useless but was positively dangerous. Truly, 'men are but children of a larger growth.'"

Harry Turner is mostly forgotten today, but those who know where to look can find his legacy in Forest Park. The statue there of St. Francis of Assisi was commissioned by Alice Turner and installed in 1962. Mrs. Turner felt that her late husband "resembled St. Francis in his love for humanity and simple natural things."

The cover of the March 18, 1915 Easter issue of Harry Turner's magazine *Much Ado*, published from his office on Delmar. Courtesy State Historical Society of Missouri.

An image of the St. Francis of Assisi statue in Forest Park. Courtesy Forest Park Forever.

To fuel the horseless carriages powered by internal combustion engines, gasoline was purchased in open containers from blacksmiths, pharmacies, and hardware stores until 1905, when the Automobile Gasoline Company, a subsidiary of the Shell Oil Company, built a gas station at 420 South Theresa in St. Louis. The station required customers to do nearly all the work—carry a five-gallon fuel can to a gas pump behind the store, fill the can, and then carry the can back to their vehicle and fill its tank—but the station was the very first in the United States built for fueling road vehicles, once again making St. Louis a gateway city in transportation.

The first operational automotive gas station in St. Louis, opened in 1905 at 420 South Theresa. Courtesy Missouri History Museum, St. Louis.

The former gas station at 420 South Theresa once its tanks had been removed. Courtesy Missouri History Museum, St. Louis.

By 1916, gas stations, such as this one operated by the Pierce Oil Company at 4614 Washington Boulevard, had become not just more user-friendly but even stylish.

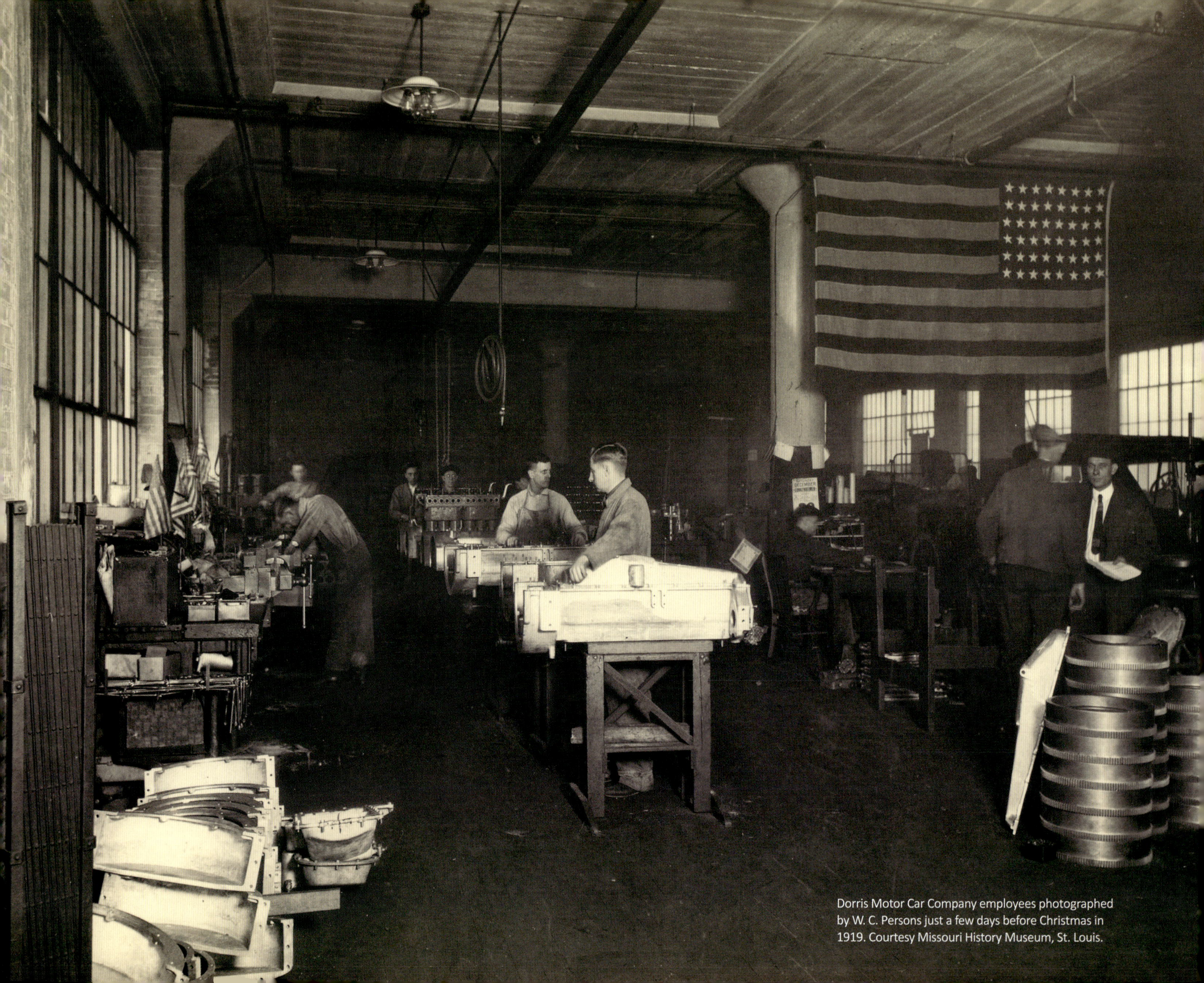

Dorris Motor Car Company employees photographed by W. C. Persons just a few days before Christmas in 1919. Courtesy Missouri History Museum, St. Louis.

BUILDING BOOM

The turn of the twentieth century saw an explosion of automobile development across the country, and St. Louis was no exception. Entrepreneurs, dreamers, and businessmen of varying levels of experience and expertise organized firms to manufacture and sell the invention that would revolutionize travel in coming decades. Many of these will be familiar to the reader, but an even larger number of firms didn't get past the filing stage. Of those that did, many wound up selling automobiles, not manufacturing them. The roster of St. Louis firms that reached the filing stage is a long one.

In a happy coincidence, perhaps inspired by Henry Borbein's early success, neighboring businessman Gustavus von Brecht of Brecht Butchers' Supply Company at 1209 Cass Avenue decided in 1901 he wanted to enter the automotive manufacturing world. The two men struck an agreement: Borbein would manage Brecht Automobile Company and supply the chassis and bodies, while Brecht would supply the steam and electric power plants. A 1902 patent filed by Borbein with Brecht as the assignor demonstrates not only the design and engineering of the shared vehicle creation, but also new corporate ties between the two men. The Brecht Motor Car Corporation offered four different styles of bodies for their cars as well as a delivery wagon, with prices ranging from $1,200 to $1,775. Many Brecht vehicles were sold overseas through distributorships in Buenos Aires, Argentina, and Frankfort, Germany. In October 1903, Borbein bought Brecht's shares in the company and changed its name to Borbein Automobile Company while promising to fill all standing Brecht orders. The Brecht Butchers' Supply building on Cass Avenue was damaged by fire in the early twenty-first century and was demolished.

This patent of 1902 demonstrates the partnership between Gus von Brecht and Henry Borbein.

Brecht steam car, owned and driven by James Livingston in Hawera, New Zealand, 1903. The car was built by local assembler A. W. Reid; this is one of three steam cars he assembled that year. Courtesy Jim Livingston.

Just a couple of months after the Century Manufacturing Company began building automobiles on South Second Street in St. Louis in the spring of 1901, a fire in the building rendered $7,500 in damages and forced the company to close. Little is known about the Century vehicles, and none are known to survive.

The Neustadt-Perry Company, founded by J. H. Neustadt and his business partner R. E. Perry in 1901 after opening a location at 826–830 South Eighteenth Street, began with the construction and sale of steam motor cars and steam and gas engine parts, specializing in carburetors. The Automobile Review of February 20, 1904, raved of Neustadt-Perry, "The running gear, bodies, and engines are well known throughout the trade, and already possess an enviable reputation." Their vehicle bodies, designed in the King of Belgium style, were built of ash and yellow poplar, and the engines they supplied ranged from four to forty horsepower. Neustadt bought out Perry in 1904 and continued as first the J. H. Neustadt Company and then, in 1906, as the Neustadt Automobile and Supply Company. While Neustadt continued to build just a few cars, the company's main business was selling kits and smaller pieces such as hardware and trimmings. It began building commercial trucks around 1910 and even built three four-wheel drive automobiles in 1915. Neustadt retired in 1917 and moved to California.

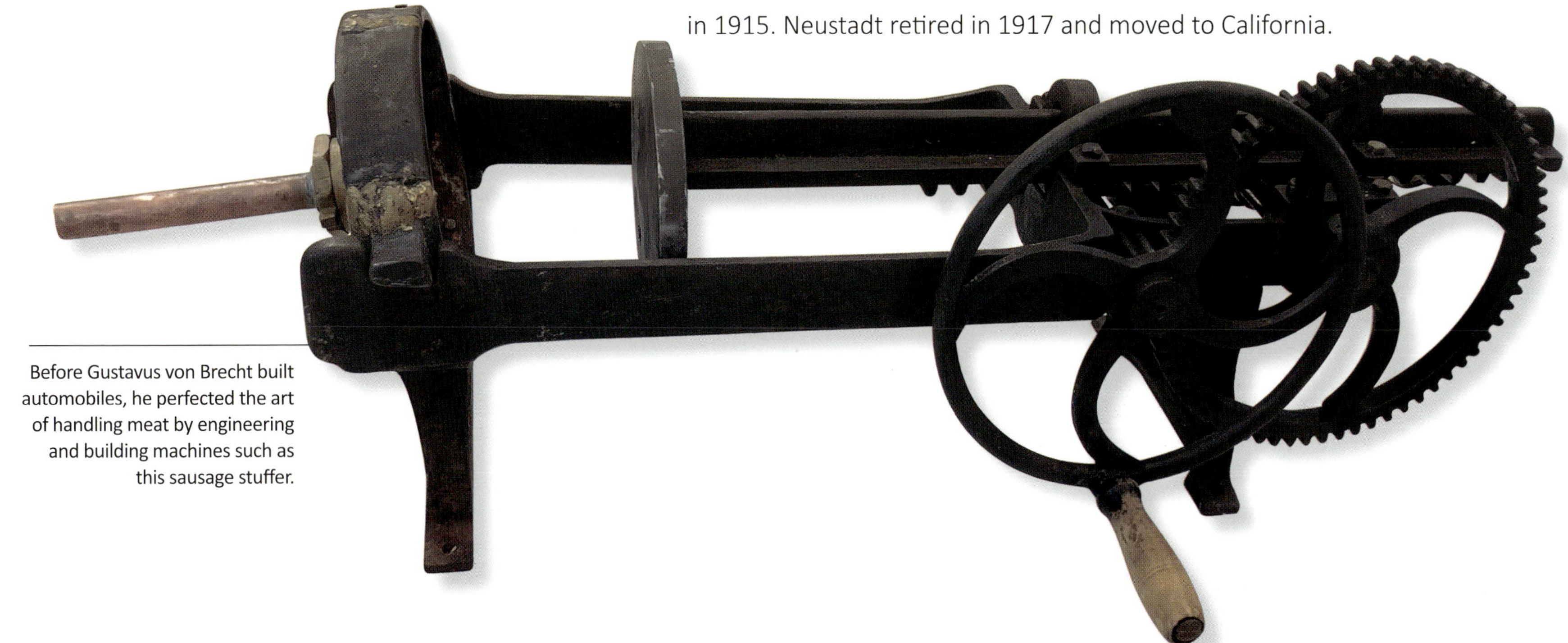

Before Gustavus von Brecht built automobiles, he perfected the art of handling meat by engineering and building machines such as this sausage stuffer.

1904

Incorporated in late May 1904 with a capital stock of $100,000 and an unfortunately apt name, the Lemon Automobile and Manufacturing Company opened its offices in the then-new Frisco building at Ninth and Olive streets in downtown St. Louis. It bought Edward Bauls' billiard hall at 3419 Lindell Boulevard for its factory building. Lemon offered only one style of vehicle known as the Meteor surrey, built in a two-seat buckboard style. The company remained in business for only one year, and none of its vehicles are known to survive.

1905

Seizing upon the popularity of high-wheeled automobiles in the age before many roads were paved, the Auto Buggy Manufacturing Company utilized two-passenger runabout, three-passenger tonneau, and touring car bodies in their drawings. Capitalizing on the success of the American Brewing Company, or ABC Beers, founded by the St. Louis

Advertisement for the A.B.C. automobile, circa 1908.

brewing family Koehler in 1890, Auto Buggy engineer Amedee B. Cole changed Auto Buggy's name to his own initials, A. B. C. Motor Vehicle Manufacturing Company. The company's first vehicle was released in 1906 with "an air-cooled engine, friction transmission . . . and 36-inch tires." Cole advertised his product was "the cheapest high-grade car in America" and was "as simple as you can guess to operate." In 1908, he was able to sell 183 automobiles from his factory along the 3900 block of Morgan Street, and in 1909, both two- and four-cylinder engines with the Cole bevel roller transmission were offered. However, he owed his suppliers $1,070 by 1910, and he filed for bankruptcy and closed his company in December of that year. Only three vehicles built by A. B. C. Motor are known to exist.

O. H. Van Kleck knew money could be made by selling both simple two-cylinder gasoline automobiles as well as parts for vehicles when he started the Crescent Automobile and Supply Company in his home at 2254 Missouri Avenue in St. Louis in the early summer of 1905.

First home of the Crescent Automobile and Supply Company.

Front-wheel-drive drivetrain built by the Auto Front-Drive Manufacturing Company.

But his true passion was designing and selling race cars, and Crescent offered only one road vehicle, with either a roadster body with a 96-inch wheelbase or a touring body with a 100-inch wheelbase. Only a few were built, and Kleck returned to selling only parts. His brick house still stands.

In the fall of 1905, at 2821 Easton Avenue in St. Louis, the Auto Front-Drive Manufacturing Company began the production of a front-drive axle for automobiles in an era in which almost all vehicles were driven by the rear axle and some four-wheel-drive. The company had tested its new chain-driven axle for months in a vehicle it had built for that specific purpose and advertised its axle could "pull your automobile same as a team of horses." Beck & Corbett's Iron Company handled the sales of the axles.

1907 Moon Model C advertisement. The model's retail price began at $3,500. Courtesy Missouri History Museum, St. Louis.

The Moon factory building at Main and Cornelia streets in 1927. Courtesy Missouri History Museum, St. Louis.

It took only one horse, a bridle, and a saddle—gifts from his parents for his twenty-first birthday—for Joseph W. Moon to start building his own road, one that would lead through one of St. Louis's great automotive chapters. Moon left the family farm in Brown County, Ohio, with that horse and headed west. He first worked as a traveling photographer, but in 1875 became a salesman for a large buggy company based along the East Coast. In 1882, Joseph and his brother John started the Moon Brothers Buggy Company in St. Louis, and by 1888, the company was selling over five thousand carriages and wagons each year.

Sensing an evolution of equine to engine power was beginning, Joseph sold his half of the carriage company to his brother in 1893 and created the Joseph W. Moon Buggy Company. After attending a carriagemakers' convention in Detroit in 1902, Moon decided to step into the automotive manufacturing world and divided his St. Louis factory into wagon and automotive divisions. His first automobile, called the "Hercules" in its early days and renamed the "Moon Model A," was built in 1905 and debuted at the New York Automobile Show in January 1906. Designed by former Peerless engineer Louis P. Mooers, the five-passenger touring car with a Roi des Belges body featured a thirty to thirty-five horsepower Rutenber engine, a three-speed sliding gear transmission, and a shaft drive. Priced at $3,000, the vehicle was targeted to the luxury segment, and forty-five were built for the 1906 model year, leading to the incorporation of the Moon Motor Car Company.

Moon began his automotive pioneering vein by designing aluminum-coated steel bodies in 1907 and offering them in 1908 and 1909, but the associated costs pushed the company back to steel composite bodies in 1910. Moon also created the dual-cowl touring or "phaeton" body in 1916 and was one of the few companies to use the fabric-covered Childs System bodies in the mid-1920s.

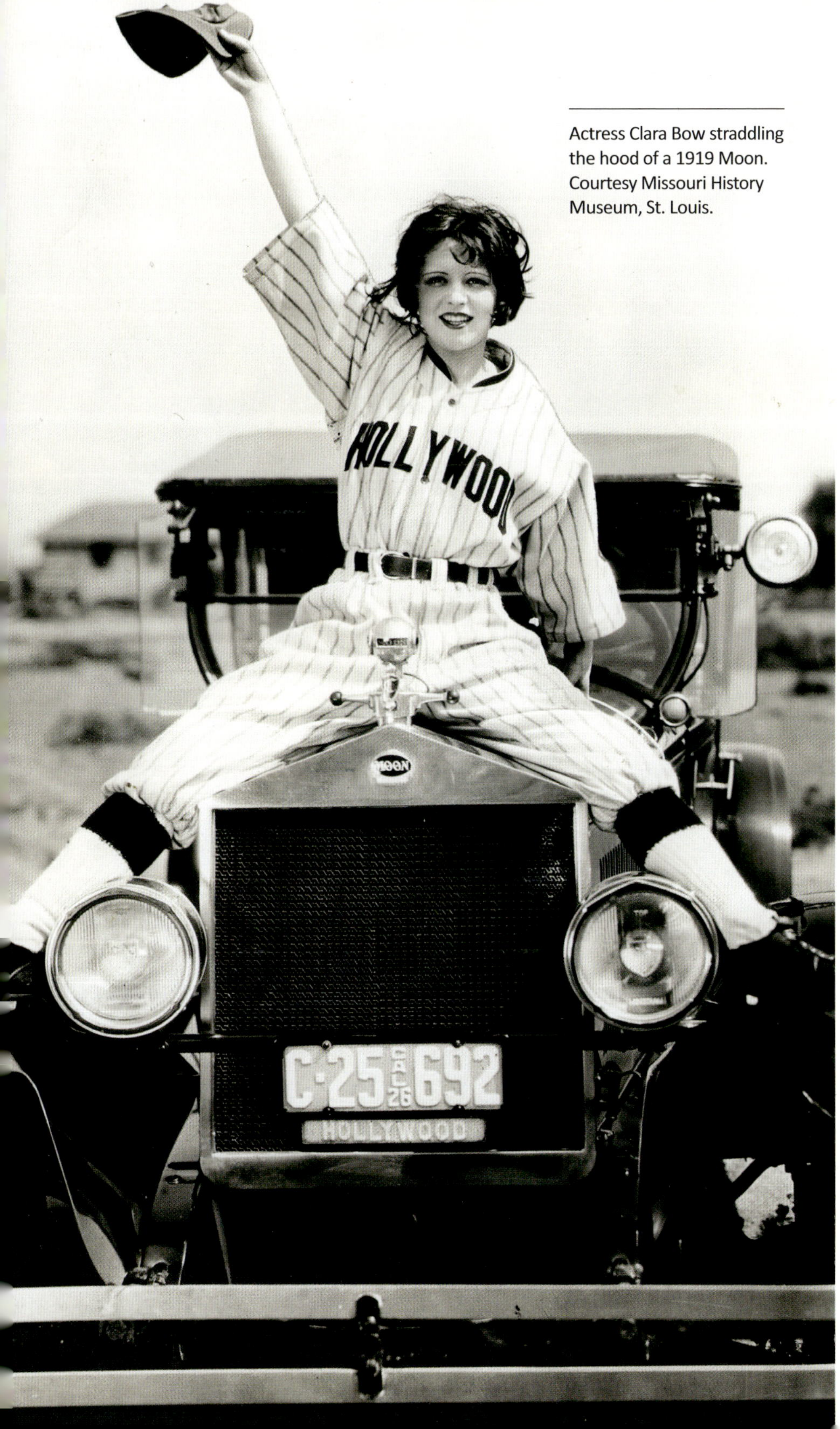

Actress Clara Bow straddling the hood of a 1919 Moon. Courtesy Missouri History Museum, St. Louis.

By 1910, Moon had reduced the prices of its vehicles to $1,500 and $2,000. In 1913, when the first six-cylinder Moons arrived, the company sold over 1,500 vehicles. By 1916, most Moons featured L-head Continental six-cylinder engines, although exported 6-42 models included Falls overhead valve engines.

Moon continued to build carriages alongside motor vehicles through 1916, and when Joseph Moon died in 1919, the presidency of Moon Motor Car Company passed to son-in-law Stewart MacDonald, even though two of Moon's own sons worked for the company.

MacDonald continued his late father-in-law's tradition of innovation and by the mid-1920s had incorporated balloon tires, hydraulic brakes, and demountable rims on wheels easily detachable from the axles. Moon reached its peak production year in 1925, with over thirteen thousand vehicles built. That same year, it introduced the stylish "Diana" line, which only lasted until 1928. By then, sales had begun to plummet. That year, Carl W. Burst Sr. took over management of the company, and in January 1929, a straight-eight touring car with the make name

Moon Motor Car Company
St. Louis, Missouri

Five-Passenger Royal Roadster
Five-Passenger Royal Cabriolet Roadster
Five-Passenger Royal Two-Door Sedan
Five-Passenger Royal Four-Door Sedan
Five-Passenger Standard Two-Door Sedan
Five-Passenger Standard Four-Door Sedan
(Prices upon application)

Moon Four-Door Sedan — 6-72

Color	Optional
Seating	Five
Wheelbase	120 inches
Wheels	Wood
Tires	29 x 5.50 inches, balloon
Brakes	Foot, hydraulic, contracting on four wheels; Hand, contracting on transmission
Engine	Six cylinder, vertical, cast in block, 3⅜x4 inches; head removable; valves in side; horsepower 27.3 N.A.C.C. rating
Lubrication	Force feed and splash
Crankshaft	Seven bearing
Radiator	Cellular
Cooling	Water pump
Ignition	Storage battery
Starter	Two unit
Fuel Feed	Vacuum
Clutch	Single plate
Speeds	Three forward, one reverse
Drive	Spiral bevel
Rear Springs	Semi-elliptic
Rear Axle	Semi-floating
Steering	Cam and lever

Standard Equipment—Transmission theft lock, rear view mirror, stop light, oil and gasoline gauges on instrument board, shock absorbers, electric horn, cowl ventilator, spare tire carrier, headlight dimmer, speedometer, ammeter, demountable rims, automatic windshield cleaner. Closed cars have dome light.

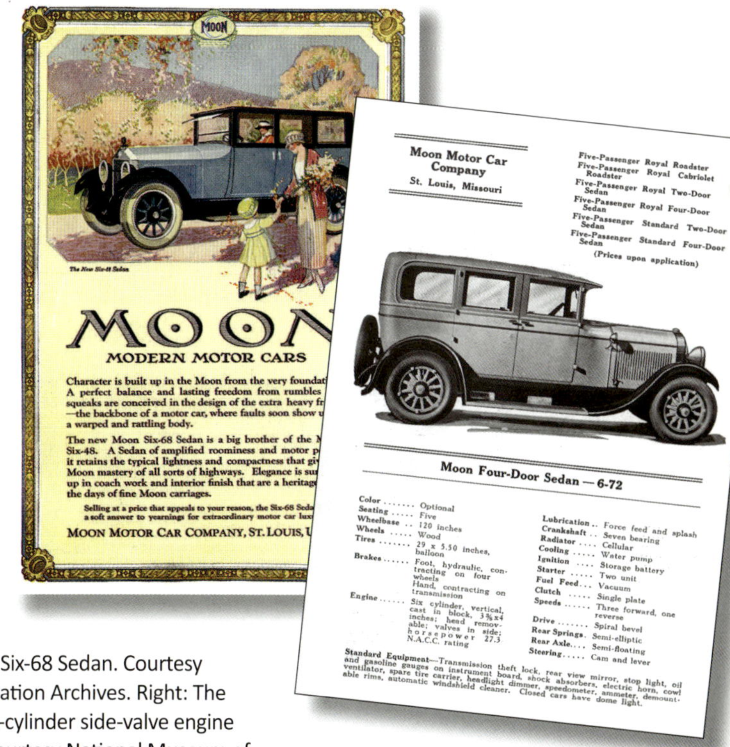

Left: An ad for the 1920 Moon Six-68 Sedan. Courtesy National Museum of Transportation Archives. Right: The 1928 Moon 6-72 featured a six-cylinder side-valve engine capable of 27.3 horsepower. Courtesy National Museum of Transportation Archives.

1928 Diana built by Moon. Courtesy Missouri History Museum, St. Louis.

1928 Moon five-passenger. Courtesy Missouri History Museum, St. Louis.

1929 Moon photographed by Paramount Commercial Studios in St. Louis. Courtesy Missouri History Museum, St. Louis.

1929 Windsor White Prince Full Sedan built by Moon. Courtesy Missouri History Museum, St. Louis.

"Windsor" was introduced. By the spring of 1929, the Moon name disappeared entirely, having been replaced by Windsor, but the crash of the American stock market that autumn hurt the depressed sales of the Windsor even more. Looking for a way to save the company, Burst and the Moon management seized upon an idea offered by independent automotive investor Archie Andrews to produce a low-slung, front-wheel-drive Cord competitor, the Ruxton, featuring a body by Edward G. Budd Manufacturing of Philadelphia. Though Peerless,

1929 Ruxton built by Moon
Courtesy Detroit Public Library.

1932 Ruxton, one of only five painted in the
Joseph Irving striped scheme.
Courtesy Cartype.

Marmon, and Gardner turned down the opportunity to build the Ruxton, Moon traded a controlling percentage of its company's stocks to Andrews in exchange for the Ruxton patents and design. However, Andrews had made a similar deal with the Kissel Company of Hartford, Wisconsin. In April 1930, Andrews, with the assistance of a court order and St. Louis police officers, forcibly overtook the Moon Motor Car Company from Burst and other members of Moon's management, who had barricaded themselves in the Moon plant. Just 96 Ruxtons were built in the St. Louis and Hartford plants, and Moon declared bankruptcy and closed its doors in November 1930. Its factory was sold for $72,000 cash just a few years later to the Cupples Company for the production of matches. Only nineteen Ruxtons are known to survive.

While Moon built and showed an automobile before its motor car company was officially created, the Victor Motor Car Company opened shop at 3938 Laclede Avenue in St. Louis in 1905 but didn't begin selling vehicles until 1907. It began by offering four different body styles—runabouts, four-passenger touring cars, Victor Pullmans, and delivery wagons—ranging in price from $450 to $800. All were chain driven by two-cylinder, two-cycle, water-cooled engines capable of producing between fourteen and sixteen horsepower. The following year, Victor moved to air-cooled engines and continued to market the vehicles as "hand forged" and the "strongest machine built," featuring construction in which "everything is doubled," including double chains, double brakes, double ignition systems, and double coils. In 1909, the company offered both water- and air-cooled engines; for the 1912 model year, nine different body types were available on Victors ranging in price from $950 for the Style D two-cylinder convertible or surrey with twenty to twenty-four horsepower to $2,000

for the Victor 40 body styles featuring four-cylinder motors with forty horsepower. Despite Victor's reincorporation as the Victor Automobile Manufacturing Company in 1910, quintupling its capital stock value from $30,000 to $150,000, and the ambitious model offering for 1912, Victor closed shop in late 1911.

A builder that technically never opened shop was the Bagnall Automobile Company, incorporated by Henry B. Graham, William F. Bagnall, and James E. Morse in 1905 with a capital investment of $10,000. The three men fancied designing and building automobiles, but they quickly determined instead to sell Cadillacs from the company's dealership at 4152 Olive Street.

1907 Victor Auto Buggy.

Lakedel Automobile Company ad for Jackson Motor Cars and the Car DeLuxe, 1908 Gould's *St. Louis City Directory*.

Lakedel's ad for the Pennsylvania Wayne and its "motraobility." Courtesy *St. Louis Post-Dispatch*, March 31, 1907.

Lakedel's listing among dealers for the Pennsylvania Auto Motor Company. Courtesy Auto Review.

Just months later, the Lakedel Automobile Company traveled a road very similar to Bagnall's. Founded by prominent businessmen W. J. Rea, J. A. Prescott, and G. B. O'Reilly, the firm was capitalized with $15,000 in 1906. Located at 5143 Delmar Boulevard, the firm didn't ever produce an automobile, but by 1907 it was selling the Pennsylvania Wayne automobiles and became a distributor for Jackson Motor Cars in 1908. By 1909, this location was home to the Gardner Motor Car Company.

After building and selling railroad cars and streetcars at its 5000-block

1907 American Mors. Courtesy Detroit Public Library.

An American Mors competing in the 1907 Giant's Despair Hill Climb in Wilkes-Barre, Pennsylvania. Courtesy Detroit Public Library.

four to thirty-two horsepower for $5,000, and a forty to fifty-two horsepower touring car for $6,000—for three years and then decided to introduce its own Standard Six design in 1909. Available as a touring car, a roadster, or a miniature tonneau on a 124-inch wheelbase, the Standard Six featured a six-cylinder engine with fifty horsepower, a three-speed transmission, a shaft drive transmission, a dual-system ignition with a Remy High-Speed magneto, and a top speed of 65 miles per hour for $3,000. For 1911, a limousine with a $4,000 price was added. The company then refinanced and decided to stop building automobiles but remained in the railcar manufacturing industry until 1974.

Like St. Louis Car Company, another large St. Louis company decided to officially enter the automotive world in 1906. After seeing an exhibit of two dozen two-ton commercial trucks at the 1904 World's Fair in St. Louis, the management of the Anheuser-Busch Brewing Association realized the value of motorized vehicles as marketing tools and began using trucks as mobile

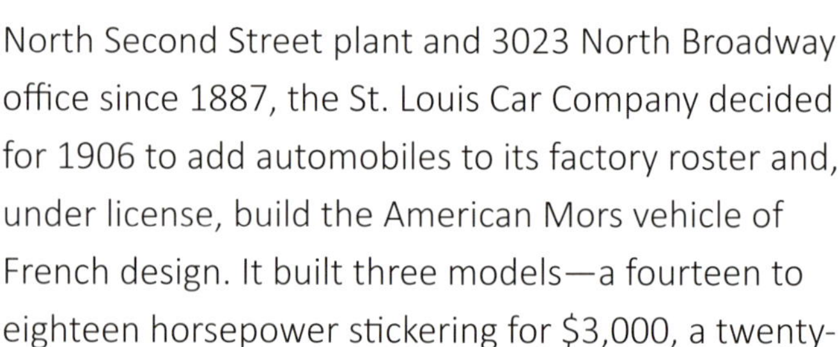

North Second Street plant and 3023 North Broadway office since 1887, the St. Louis Car Company decided for 1906 to add automobiles to its factory roster and, under license, build the American Mors vehicle of French design. It built three models—a fourteen to eighteen horsepower stickering for $3,000, a twenty-

An Anheuser-Busch wagon being built in the company's shop on Pestalozzi Street in 1900. Courtesy Missouri History Museum, St. Louis.

billboards. However, the challenges of operating and maintaining motorized vehicles nearly convinced the company in the winter of 1905 to abandon using them altogether and revert to horse-drawn equipment.

The company decided to take a new approach for 1906 and, in January of that year, hired Charles O. Marian, a well-known and respected local gasoline and electric motor mechanic, to oversee the newly defined Anheuser-Busch Brewing Association Vehicle Department. Thanks to Marian's knowledge and discipline, as well as a charging garage capable of holding sixty large electric delivery trucks, the Anheuser-Busch fleet, previously known as "white elephants," achieved remarkable reliability standards. Automotive enthusiast Adolphus Busch rode the success of his company's vehicle department to have it build bus bodies, refrigerated truck bodies, armored vehicle bodies, and recreational vehicles, including the Lampsteed Kampkar, designed around a Model T in 1920, for commercial sale. Busch was also intrigued by a boat on wheels making the auto show circuits. Designed in the custom-body division of Manhattan Willys-Overland and Peerless distributor Conover T. Silver, the vehicle featured a twelve-foot-long boat body on an Overland chassis and was shown all over the country. After it was used in the 1916 film Gloria's Romance, Anheuser-Busch bought the vehicle, created a slightly updated and larger design based on it, and contracted to build it as an amphibious reconnaissance vehicle for World War I. This inboard land cruiser didn't go into production until the war had ended in 1918, so the brewery converted it to promotional use for Liberty Loan war bond drives, military recruitment and recognition, and as the "Bevo Boat" to market the brewery's non-alcoholic beer. Records indicate but

Top: 1930 Budweiser II Landcruiser. Courtesy Greg R. Rhomberg, Antique Warehouse. Left: An angled view of one of the Anheuser-Busch boat cars taken in Tower Grove Park in 1931. Courtesy Missouri History Museum, St. Louis. Right: The left side of a Budweiser boat car.

do not prove a total of eight cars of four different series were built on Pierce-Arrow chassis with Continental Big Six motors, and all had boat-like bell and snout front ends, rudders, propellers, anchors, harbor lights, and even life jackets. Renamed the Budweiser Beer car after Prohibition ended in 1933, the cars were taken on national tours, and one is known to survive, although it now has a chassis from a 1930 V-12 Cadillac Sport Phaeton.

George Preston Dorris probably didn't need Anheuser-Busch's mobile marketing to persuade him to re-enter the automotive manufacturing world. After the family of his late partner John French moved the St. Louis Motor Carriage Company to Peoria, Illinois, in 1905—two years following John's death in Pittsburgh—Dorris decided to open the Dorris Motor Car Company in 1906. Assisted by the investment of grocer Harry B. Krenning, he utilized the former St. Louis Motor Carriage plant at 1211–13 North Vandeventer for his new company. Krenning was named the company's first president, and Dorris hit the ground running with its innovative 1906 Dorris.

Introduced at the New York Auto Show in January 1906, the Dorris featured roller bearings invented and built by the Timken Roller Bearing and Axle Company, founded by St. Louis carriage maker Henry Timken and his sons in 1899, a body-on-frame construction, and the first use of a four-cylinder motor in an automobile. Those features, as well as the vehicle's hand-built construction and detailed design, helped it command a sticker price of $2,500 and earn rave reviews. In its October 1907 issue, *Auto Review* stated, "The wonderful success of the Dorris car this past season, which was its first appearance on the American automobile market, was so pronounced and gave St. Louis such a proud distinction for having manufactured such an excellent automobile, that the coming season for this car means that the Dorris Motor Car Co. will be able to sell all the cars they can build. This car has a wonderful record for reliability, endurance and for the least cost of maintenance in the East, Middle West and Far West. All hail the 1907 Dorris!"[1]

Advertisement for the introduction of the 1906 Dorris at New York and Chicago auto shows.

1903 St. Louis. Courtesy National Museum of Transportation Archives.

---

1 *Auto Review*, October 1907, page 45.

George Dorris felt he should know every customer and was willing to build any car they wanted over the Dorris chassis. Courtesy Dorris Family Collection.

Dorris sales quickly achieved volumes too big for the old St. Louis Motor Carriage plant. Krenning hired St. Louis architect John L. Wees, who in 1902 had designed a mercantile building for Krenning's wholesale grocery business, to draw plans to meet Dorris's specifications at 22–38 South Sarah Street. Completed in 1907, the two-story brick building with iron columns was nearly fireproof and featured an assembly room, machine shop, blacksmith shop, and offices on its first floor, while the painting and finishing room, trimming room, and woodworking area were included on the second floor. The building also included an automotive industry first—testing areas in which an entire engineering department evaluated components for quality and durability.

The year 1909 brought not only the innovative transmission-geared speedometer, yet another first in the industry, to Dorris but also a third story to its Sarah Street plant. After introducing an electric self-starter in 1911—one year before Cadillac—the company expanded yet again in 1912 by spending $100,000 to build a three-story factory and showroom building just to the west of the existing plant. Movement of assembly to the new building allowed Dorris to utilize the 1907 building for automobile service and repair.

Dorris plant number two at the northeast corner of Forest Park Avenue and South Sarah Street. Courtesy National Museum of Transportation Archives. Inset: The Dorris plant on Forest Park Avenue was completed in time to house the construction and sales of the 1913 models. Courtesy Dorris Family Collection.

The Dorris Motor Car Company's plant at 4100 Laclede, designed by John Ludwig Wees, completed in 1912, and later home to Lindburg Cadillac. Courtesy Missouri History Museum, St. Louis.

Dorris took pride in its homegrown engines and transmissions. Courtesy Dorris Family Collection.

The 1913 models were the first built in the new building but, like most of their predecessors, were built entirely by hand with Dorris components. A six-cylinder motor with a distillator to remove heavy petroleum residue from gasoline before reaching the engine was introduced in the 1916 Dorris, and the car held the record for fuel economy in its weight class for three years.

Val Kloepper and George Dorris discussing the design of Dorris Motor vehicles to come on February 22, 1918. Courtesy National Museum of Transportation Archives.

A 1915 Dorris Model 1-A Six. Courtesy National Museum of Transportation Archives.

CIC@CET

Left and Above: The Dorris Motor Car Company plant and showroom at what is now 4059–4065 Forest Park Avenue, completed in 1907.

output shrank so dramatically that by 1921, only three vehicles were being produced in the plant each week. Stockholders voted to liquidate the Dorris Motor Car Company in 1923, but a circuit court blocked the liquidation to prevent primarily benefiting Kenning. The company was then dissolved in 1926 after building 3,044 cars and 909 trucks during its two decades of existence.[2] George Dorris started a new gear manufacturing company that is still in business almost a century later, and three Cadillac dealerships and lofts utilized the former Dorris Motor Car Company building, which is today home to the Center for Emerging Technologies.

John C. Higdon and J. Garretson Higdon served as president and vice president, respectively, of the Success Auto Buggy Manufacturing Company. (John Higdon was a patent lawyer who had built a one-off vehicle in 1896.) The company's office and manufacturing facility were located on DeBaliviere Avenue near the city's fashionable Central West End neighborhood.

The Dorris Model 6-80. Courtesy National Museum of Transportation Archives.

While each vehicle leaving his plant upheld both George Dorris' belief that cars should be timeless and his marketing slogan, "Built Up to a Standard—Not Down to a Price," those prices began to drive consumers to cheaper vehicles built on assembly lines. While Dorris reorganized, added construction of trucks and buses, and acquired the Mogul Motor Truck Company during World War I to help offset declines in sales,

---

2 *The Auto Review. A Monthly Publication Devoted to the Interests of Owners and Manufacturers of Automobiles, Motor Cycles, and Boats.* St. Louis, November 1907. Pages 1, 12–13.

In summer 1915, Cory N. and Laura N. Smith drove their 1910 Dorris from St. Louis to San Francisco and took this photo in the Nevada desert. Courtesy Missouri History Museum, St. Louis.

1921 Dorris Model 6-80 touring.

The Dorris commercial vehicle plant #3 on December 20, 1919. Courtesy Missouri History Museum, St. Louis.

Dorris used this three-and-a-half-ton truck for marketing. Courtesy Dorris Family Collection.

A Dorris Model 6-80 seven-passenger sedan in San Francisco, California, in 1920. Courtesy Shorpy.

Advertisement for the 1914 Dorris touring. Courtesy Missouri History Museum, St. Louis.

A specially-designed 1918 Dorris Town Car on an IC6 chassis. Courtesy Missouri History Museum, St. Louis.

1919 Dorris Model 6-80. Courtesy Missouri History Museum, St. Louis.

1921 Dorris Model 6-80 seven-passenger touring car in service as car "A" for St. Louis Fire Department Chief William Panzer. Courtesy Missouri History Museum, St. Louis.

The St. Louis Fire Department's 1918 Dorris IBW hose and chemical car. Courtesy Missouri History Museum, St. Louis. Inset: The 1907 Success Auto Buggy ad in the Gould's City Directory.

The former Dorris showroom and plant at 4100 Laclede, photographed in 2017.

The Success Auto Buggy itself was extremely low-priced was extremely low-priced for its time ($250 for the basic vehicle, $25 extra if you wanted a top!), but was, after all, truly a motorized buggy. The firm lasted from 1906 to 1909, when its arguably obsolete vehicle left the scene. The location today is home to Crossroads College Preparatory School.

Daniel Haydock and his brothers Charles and Winters went from building carriages on North Broadway to building automobiles in 1907 at their factory located at the corner of Pine and Commercial. With Daniel as president, Charles as sales manager, and Winters as the designer and superintendent, the D. W. Haydock Motor Car Company initially built the "Haydock Front Drive" in 1907.

The Dorris 6-80 was deemed tough enough to serve the United States military. Courtesy the Dorris Family Collection.

The South Sarah Street Dorris plant being used to its full capacity before moving to a new building in 1912. Courtesy Dorris Family Collection.

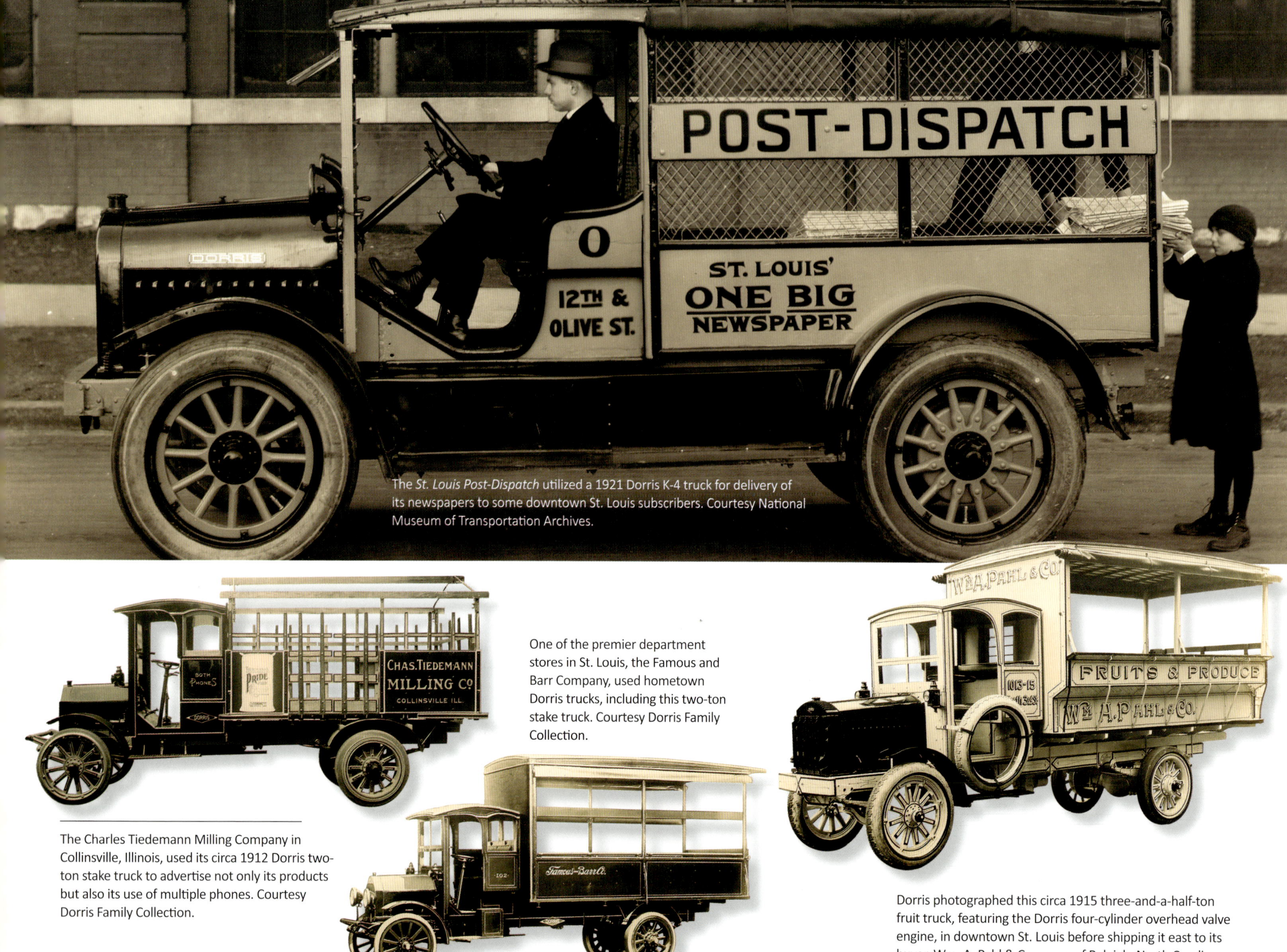

The *St. Louis Post-Dispatch* utilized a 1921 Dorris K-4 truck for delivery of its newspapers to some downtown St. Louis subscribers. Courtesy National Museum of Transportation Archives.

One of the premier department stores in St. Louis, the Famous and Barr Company, used hometown Dorris trucks, including this two-ton stake truck. Courtesy Dorris Family Collection.

The Charles Tiedemann Milling Company in Collinsville, Illinois, used its circa 1912 Dorris two-ton stake truck to advertise not only its products but also its use of multiple phones. Courtesy Dorris Family Collection.

Dorris photographed this circa 1915 three-and-a-half-ton fruit truck, featuring the Dorris four-cylinder overhead valve engine, in downtown St. Louis before shipping it east to its buyer, Wm. A. Pahl & Company of Raleigh, North Carolina. Courtesy Dorris Family Collection.

The shape of this custom Dorris screams "speed." Courtesy Dorris Family Collection.

Boys out on the town in their Dorris 6-80 hardtop cabriolet. Courtesy Dorris Family Collection.

Dorris in front of Brookings Hall. Courtesy Missouri History Museum, St. Louis.

Building chauffeur-driven limousines was not unusual for Dorris. Courtesy Dorris Family Collection.

1907

By 1909 the firm had switched to the Cosmopolitan, a lower-priced entry in the motorized vehicle market at $350. One source describes this vehicle as a "spindly high-wheeler" without fenders. Perhaps its demise shouldn't surprise us. By 1915 the Haydock Brothers Carriage Company had moved to 401 Olive Boulevard, and by 1920 it was gone. The Haydock brothers lived together at 5975 Cote Brilliante and, while the home still stands, it is abandoned like so many other city properties.

Dr. Isaac H. Cadwallader, Physician in Charge of the Missouri Baptist Sanitarium, found time to serve as the president of the Eureka Motor Buggy Company in 1909. (Dr. Cadwallader's wife, Ella, served as the Sanitarium superintendent.) John Woodburn served as vice president and C. C. Allen as treasurer. Initially located at 4500 Morgan in the Laclede's Landing area, the firm moved west to 3025–27 Olive Street by 1910. The firm's high-wheeler was designed by Charles Zimmerman, who has been described as the "moving force" of the company.

Although some sources indicate the firm was gone after 1910, the 1911 St. Louis City Directory shows both the Eureka Motor Car Manufacturing Company and the Eureka Auto Parts Manufacturing Company at the Olive Street location. While the firm's motor buggies were phased out, the auto parts manufacturing operation continued on for several years under new leadership and at a new location at 1915–17 Pine Street.

The optimistically named "Everybody's" automobile was a low-priced runabout. At a $450 price point, the Everybody's was within the reach of more households than many of its competitors. The Everybody's Motor Car Manufacturing Company seems to have had several locations in its short life; a 1907 advertisement lists 401 North Broadway as its home, while the 1908 St. Louis City Directory gives an address of 1720 North Second Street.

Unfortunately, the Everybody's vehicle wasn't everybody's cup of tea, and the firm was gone by 1909. However, one of its cars survives. W. J. Seufert, owner of the Seufert Brothers Cannery of The Dalles, Oregon, ordered a 1907

A current Zillow image of the former Haydock home at 5975 Cote Brilliante.

Eureka Motor Buggy image in the December 1907 issue of *The Automobile*.

Eureka Auto Parts Manufacturing's ad in the 1920 *Gould's Business Directory*.

Everybody's and was disappointed when it arrived by rail in crates and boxes. He hired a mechanic to assemble it, and the family kept it operational until the 1950s. They donated it to the Western Antique Aeroplane and Automobile Museum in Hood River, Oregon, where it remains.

The Winner Motor Buggy Company produced just what the name suggests: a motorized buggy. Most sources suggest that the Winner Motor Buggy Company lasted from 1907 to 1909.

However, a tag affixed to the 1903 Winner pictured indicates that it is a product of the Winner Manufacturing Company of East St. Louis, Illinois.

The 1904 St. Louis City Directory lists the Cook Brothers Carriage Company as "successors to [the] Timken Carriage Company" on North Second Street in downtown St. Louis. Recognizing the need for a better bearing on heavy vehicles, the Timken Carriage Company evolved into the Timken Company, an international conglomerate that today employs 17,000 people across the world.

The manufacturer's tag on the 1903 Winner Motor Buggy Model R in the Penngrove Power and Implement Museum.

A 1903 Winner Motor Buggy Model R in the Penngrove Power and Implement Museum in California.

A 1907 Everybody's auto in the collections of the Western Antique Aeroplane and Automobile Museum.

The Cook Motor Vehicle Company, on the other hand, built a vehicle called the Simplo, a high-wheeler, for a single year. It was not successful, but Cook continued in the automobile painting and service business, as well as a dealer for other makes.

Fred Campbell began selling automotive parts and accessories from his store at 2806 Locust in the early years of the twentieth century, and by 1907, he was installing Goodyear solid and inflatable tires in his shop at 712–714 Morgan Street. The businesses flourished enough for him to plan to build a second branch at 3219 Locust Street, in the heart of "Automobile Row," in December of 1914, with an alley entrance to the service department in the back of the building. He ended up at 2802–2804 Locust; the site is now a parking lot.

The Jai Alai Building on DeBaliviere hosted the St. Louis auto show on December 14–21, 1907. The show—second nationally in size only to a show in Chicago—required two annexes totaling over 13,000 square feet to be added to the building for the indoor show. Participants included Moon Motor Car Company, Peper Automobile Company, South Side Auto Company, St. Louis Car Company, Logan Motor Dispatch, Colonial

The Victorian flair of the grandstands at Fairgrounds Park stood in stark contrast to the automotive races held there. F. J. Koster photographed this racer in 1907. © F. J. Koster, courtesy Missouri History Museum, St. Louis.

The "Great 24 Hours Race" at Fairgrounds Park in 1907. Courtesy Missouri History Museum, St. Louis.

Automobile Company, Mississippi Valley Automobile Company (which had the largest exhibit with nineteen cars), Park Automobile Company, Western Automobile Company, Dorris Motor Car Company, Halsey Automobile Company, and Union Electric Light & Power.[2]

A more exciting event for automotive spectators to witness the same year was the "Great 24 Hours Race" held on the former horse racing track at what would become Fairgrounds Park the following year. The site in north St. Louis had previously been privately owned and had been used as the site of the St. Louis Exposition from 1856 to 1902, excepting its use during the Civil War as the Union encampment Benton Barracks. Preparations for the 1904 World's Fair, as well as the outlawing of gambling on horse racing in Missouri in 1905, left the site dormant until the automotive race and the city's purchase and reopening of the grounds as Fairgrounds Park in 1908.

---

2 *The Auto Review. A Monthly Publication Devoted to the Interests of Owners and Manufacturers of Automobiles, Motor Cycles, and Boats.* St. Louis, November 1907. Pages 1, 12–13.

1908

A 1908 Jeannin Runabout.

The Durable Motor Car Company was a short-lived manufacturer that boasted a one-year guarantee on its "Clymer" highwheeler. Those who bought the car for its guarantee were undoubtedly disappointed to discover that the guarantee outlived the firm.

Another one-year wonder was the Jeannin Automobile and Manufacturing Company. Capitalized at $15,000, the firm was located at 1119–21 North Vandeventer Avenue and produced a highwheeler advertised as "The Car That Goes and Comes." Headed by Harry W. Jeannin, Edward Fritschle, Harry Goerner, and Oscar Milentz, the firm was out of business by 1909. However, Harry Jeannin ultimately became quite successful after receiving a patent for a new kind of alternating current motor. He formed the Jeannin Electric Company in Toledo, Ohio, which operated until his death in 1929 at age 60. The Jeannin Electric Company was then sold.

As the result of a century-old transcription error, the Haase-Bohle Carriage Company has been misidentified as the House and Rohle Carriage Company in numerous sources over the years. Headed up by Charles Haase and Frank Bohle, the firm built carriages in St. Louis for decades. Successful enough to build a new factory in 1908, the firm moved from its

The Jeannin Single Phase Repulsion Induction Motor.

BEHEN-FAUGHT MOTOR CAR EQUIPMENT CO.

In the absence of side curtains, doors, or even tops, turn-of-the-century automobile enthusiasts ("autoists") found it necessary to dress appropriately for a ride in a horseless carriage. Naturally, accessory firms sprung up to meet the demand for goggles, dusters, hats, and other equipment for the motoring public. In St. Louis, A. L. Dyke was the first, but by no means the last, to supply the autoist with clothing and other accessories. The Behen-Faught Motor Car Equipment Company at 3961 Olive Street advertised itself as a provider of "Everything for the Autoist but the Auto." The Behen-Faught Motor Car Equipment Company was succeeded by Missouri Auto Specialty Company, which changed the name of the company but kept the slogan.

A Behen-Faught Motor Car Equipment Company advertisement placed in 1908.

The former Scudder Motor Truck Building located at 3942–62 Laclede Avenue. Courtesy Preservation Resource Office.

A Scudder Service advertisement from 1920. Courtesy *St. Louis Post-Dispatch*.

original location at Eighteenth and Pine in downtown St. Louis to a tony Laclede Avenue location. Unfortunately, like so many others, the firm fell victim to the societal shift to internal combustion; by 1915 *The Automotive Manufacturer* reported that the firm's capital had fallen from $40,000 to $5,000. The building was taken over by the Scudder Motor Truck Company in 1918, which sold and serviced the Service brand of delivery and fleet trucks, and is now home to Bumper and Auto Processing of Missouri.

1909

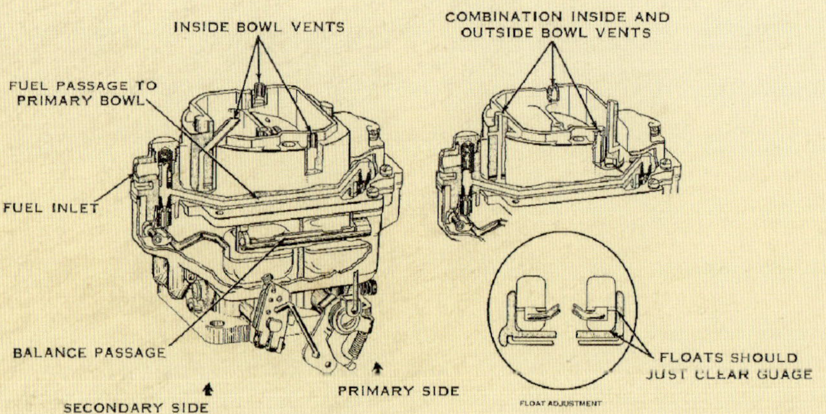

Carter Carburetor's innovative float circuit design.

The Carter Carburetor plant at 2840 North Spring Avenue in 1967. The lab building is circled. Courtesy National Building Arts Center.

After eighteen-year-old William Carter built his first carburetor in 1902, he spent seven years perfecting its design before opening Carter Carburetor with the claim of having engineered and produced the most world's most accurate carburetor, thanks in large part to precision molding. Carter also created the choke valve and downdraft design, and strong sales led him to hire noted architect Hugo K. Graf to design a factory. Completed in 1915, the four-story, 480,000-square-foot building sat on a ten-acre site at 2840 North Spring Avenue, across from the St. Louis Browns' stadium. Exactly one decade later, in 1925, the Knights of Pythias and Carter Carburetor used Graf to design a combination office, lodge hall, and parking garage at 711 North Grand. Carter used the two-story front podium section of the building as its offices until 1985; this section now serves as the Grand Center Arts Academy.

Carter supplied carburetors for a variety of automakers, including Chevrolet, Buick, Oldsmobile, Packard, Hupmobile, and Chrysler. William Carter sold the company to local railroad car builder American Car and Foundry Company (ACF) in 1924, and Carter Carburetor remained a standalone component of ACF for the following sixty years. During that time, Carter had as many

Working inside the Carter Carburetor plant in 1980. Courtesy *St. Louis Post-Dispatch*.

Carter Carburetor's administration office at 711 North Grand. Courtesy Mark Groth.

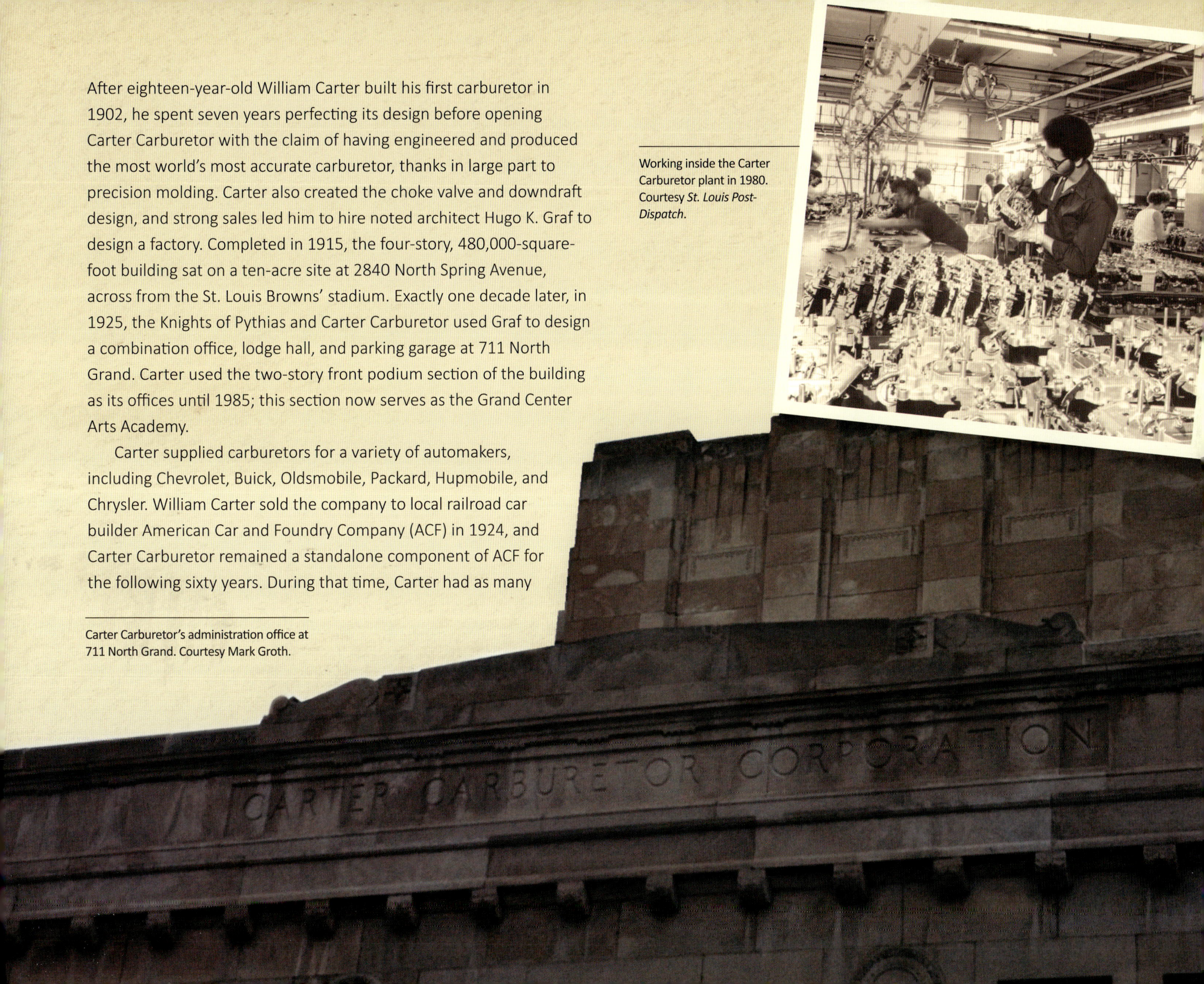

The former Carter Carburetor offices serving as the Grand Center Arts Academy. Courtesy Grand Center Arts Academy.

as 3,000 employees and created notable designs such as the Word War II Jeep's waterproofed Y-S single-barrel carburetor and the first four-barrel carburetor, introduced on Buick's straight-eight in 1952. However, the introduction of automotive fuel injection systems in the 1980s forced ACF to close Carter Carburetor and abandon the plant in 1984. The Environmental Protection Agency found polychlorinated biphenyls (PCBs), trichloroethylene (TCE), and asbestos at the site—some of which had reached bedrock thirty-five feet below topsoil—and declared the plant a Superfund site. Only after a $30 million agreement with ACF and the company managing the site was achieved in 2013 did cleanup begin. Remediation of the site was still underway as of early 2019.

The Darby Motor Car Company advertised its runabout as the "simplest automobile on earth" that "spins over the road like a monster touring car." Advertising puffery aside, the Darby was a handsome machine but unfortunately didn't make much of an impression on the motoring public. The firm only lasted two years.

"Eagle" has been a popular vehicle name since the dawn of the automobile. At least five companies built an automobile called the "Eagle" in the years before World War II. (Of course, the American Motors Corporation sold a four-wheel-drive Eagle from 1979 to 1987.) Unfortunately, none of the early Eagle manufacturers were to be successful. The Eagle Automobile Company of St. Louis lasted only one year: 1909. It quickly vanished without a trace.

An ad for the 1910 Darby Runabout.

1910

William K. Norris and Lewis E. McQuay knew they were onto something in 1910 when McQuay designed an automotive piston ring unlike any on the market. They convinced local St. Louis investor George S. Johnston to invest in the creation of McQuay-Norris Manufacturing Company and opened a shop at 1311 Chestnut Street. The company outgrew its next location on Locust Street and, in 1919, had four buildings built on Cooper—later Marconi—Street in south St. Louis's Hill neighborhood. The company continued to expand, adding piston pins, bearings, valves, water pumps, chassis and transmission parts, and other precise components for automobiles, trucks, buses, and tractors.

A McQuay-Norris teardrop test car in 1935.

Inspired by Cincinnatian John Hill's Arrow Plane, a teardrop car built on a reversed Ford Model A chassis, McQuay-Norris had the Hill Auto Body Company build six teardrop streamliners over 1933 and 1934. McQuay-Norris chose eighty-five horsepower Ford Model 18 V-8 motors to drive the streamliners from behind the rear axle, creating a center driver's area fronted by a long dashboard with fourteen specialized gauges. Behind the driver sat perhaps the most critical gauge, the blow-by meter that measured the unburned gases escaping from the engine and the effectiveness of the McQuay-Norris piston rings. Graduate engineering students drove and maintained the cars across the country from 1934 to 1940 and were able to demonstrate the quality of McQuay-Norris components to automotive repair shops and parts stores throughout the US. Only one of the six McQuay-Norris streamliners has survived.

McQuay-Norris maintained its 2320 Marconi address for its piston ring plant and administrative offices but added plants at 3260 Brannon Avenue and 6301 Manchester Road to house its expanded production and, as of 1964, 1,150 St. Louis employees. Additional plants in Indianapolis; Casey, Illinois; and Toronto, Ontario, Canada, as well as twenty-four distribution centers throughout the United States, brought the company's entire employee count to 2,100 that year. However, five years later, McQuay-Norris merged with Eaton Yale & Towne, Inc., of Toledo, Ohio.

THIS CERTIFIES

THAT YOU, *A. Jones* , ARE
(Void if not signed)
HEREBY AUTHORIZED TO WEAR THE ARMY-NAVY PRODUCTION AWARD EMBLEM in recognition of meritorious work performed as an employee of the *McQuay-Norris* company.
(Fill in name)
Part of the battle of production is being won through your efforts and this "E" emblem is visible proof of the Army's and Navy's recognition of your accomplishment. Wear it with pride.

(Signed) *Robt. P. Patterson*
Under Secretary of War

(Signed) *James Forrestal*
Under Secretary of the Navy

A World War II Army-Navy Production Award won by McQuay-Norris employee Andrew Jones for 1944–45. Courtesy Missouri History Museum, St. Louis.

1911

The Leeper Automobile Company was incorporated to great fanfare in 1911. Announcements of the firm's intent to manufacture and repair automobiles, along with the names of founders Oscar Schmidt, Stewart Leeper, and Jesse Leeper, appeared in trade publications such as *The Hub, Iron Age, and American Machinist*. Relatively thinly capitalized at $2,000, the firm does not appear to have commenced manufacturing, and did not appear in city directories the following year.

1913

Popular in the second decade of the twentieth century, cyclecars fall somewhere between motorcycles and automobiles. Light, small, and inexpensive, cyclecars would have seemed to fit the bill for someone who wanted a bit more cover than a motorcycle provides but didn't want to pay for a full-sized automobile. The Hoover Motor Company sought to exploit this market niche by producing a two-passenger, chain-driven cyclecar priced at $375. The vehicle must have been light—gas mileage of 55 mpg was claimed! Unfortunately, Hoover's cyclecar didn't catch on in St. Louis, and by 1914 the firm was gone.

CAPTAIN JOHN BERRY
AND HIS AUTOMOBILE SCHOOL

One of our city's most interesting turn-of-the-century entrepreneurs was Captain John Berry—aerialist, automobilist, educator, and all-around adventurer. He ran the Captain Berry Automobile School at the corner of Washington and Vandeventer, where he also sold Maxwell automobiles and engaged in "automobile body building, painting, and repairing." Berry's real love was ballooning; he won the first national balloon race in 1909 and engaged in many flights over the next several years. By 1915, Berry was pictured with a group of prospective balloon pilots of "Capt. John Berry's Flying Corps" who were preparing themselves for America's eventual entry into the Great War in Europe. At the age of 75, Berry piloted the lead balloon in the 1921 National Elimination race. His 1931 obituary described him as a man who was "once known as the Dean of Balloon Pilots."

Captain John Berry with his Balloon "University City" taking off just west of the Women's National Daily building in University City for the final event of the American Women's League Convention 1910. Courtesy University City Public Library.

1914

An old name in St. Louis automotive manufacturing—or, in this case, more appropriately assembly—was used in 1914 when Crescent Automobile Company formed and leased a building at Main and St. George streets for building cars with St. Louis–built bodies and assembled drivetrains. The Crescent roadster and five-passenger touring car retailed between $900 and $1,000, and the company chose tax day in 1914 for its first sale.

Manager Frank A. St. Cyr's confidence in the future growth of the Continental Auto Supply Company, based in Davenport, Iowa, was strong enough to have a "new large modern building"[3] built at 5835–39 Delmar in 1914 to handle the sales of "a full line of accessories and supplies," including everything from tires to Ford headlight regulators. The St. Louis branch stayed open through at least 1923. The Hudson-Pogue Tire Company, successor to the Pogue Auto Tire Sales Company, moved to larger quarters almost next door at 5809 Delmar the same year.[4] By the end of that decade, Delmar would become the site of St. Louis's second of three Automobile Rows.

---

[3] *Cycle and Automobile Trade Journal*, Volume 19, Chilton Company, 1914. Page 173.
[4] *The Horseless Age*, Volume 34, Horseless Age Company, August 26, 1914. Page 315.

Ford Motor Company's first St. Louis plant, 4100 Forest Park. Courtesy Missouri History Museum, St. Louis.

Several of the first Ford Model Ts built in the St. Louis plant in 1914 undergoing testing. Courtesy Missouri History Museum, St. Louis.

The City of St. Louis invested in fourteen new Ford Model Ts not long after the St. Louis plant began building them in 1914. Courtesy Missouri History Museum, St. Louis.

Ford's sales showroom in its St. Louis plant during the Depression. Courtesy Missouri History Museum, St. Louis.

Similar optimism held by another early figure in St. Louis automotive service led to an expansion with the same start date but with productions and impacts on an entirely different scale—the only way Henry Ford knew how to do things. In its early years, the Ford Motor Company utilized sales branches as opposed to dealerships to distribute its vehicles. While future St. Louis Cardinals president Samuel Breadon began selling Fords at 4701 Washington in 1903 before moving to 681 Walton to sell Pierce-Arrow and Peerless, in 1907 Johnson Automobile Company, the tenth "exclusive" Ford branch nationally, was opened in St. Louis in a rented two-story building at 3667–3669 Olive Street, a site previously used by the Macintosh Automobile Company. The first floor served as a showroom with a service entrance at the back of the building, and the second floor served as parts storage. Knowing that the exploding sales of the Model T were quickly outpacing

The former Ford plant at 4100 Forest Park Avenue adaptively reused as lofts and a pediatric urgent care facility.

production in Detroit, Ford's board of directors approved construction of a manufacturing facility at the corner of 4100 Forest Park Avenue and Sarah Street opposite the Dorris Motor Car Company plant. Ford hired St. Louis architects Clymer & Drischler, designers of an addition to the Moon Buggy plant, several factories and schools, and many high-end homes in the Central West End. The reinforced concrete building, completed in 1914, followed the same design engineering created by architect Albert Kahn for Ford's plant in Highland Park, Michigan, and allowed similar open spans to accommodate Ford's new automatic conveyor belt assembly lines. The back of the second floor was docked and doored to allow Wabash Railroad boxcars to be unloaded directly into the building. Ford sales were multiplying quickly enough for Kahn to be hired to design additions to the St. Louis plant only one year later; the addition doubled the size of the building and was completed in 1916.

From May 1917 to May 1919, the Ford factory was used by the federal government to store materials for World War I and was subsequently returned to Ford. At its peak production in 1923–24, the plant could build 325 Model Ts each day alongside assembling Ford tractors. In 1923 alone, the plant built 79,594 Model Ts and 8,281 tractors. The Great Depression reduced the building to use as a sales and service branch from 1933 to 1935. Production of the Model A resumed in January 1935, but Ford assembly ended at the Forest Park plant on February 10, 1942, in response to the United States' entry in World War II. Just three months later, the US Navy began adapting and securing the building for its use, and Ford never returned to its Forest Park plant, moving instead to acreage in Hazelwood it had purchased in 1937. The federal government sold the building to Goodwill in 1966, who owned it for twelve years before subdividing it from its adjacent building and selling it. The old plant was then used for private storage for many years. The building at 4100 Forest Park Avenue still stands; its first floor is currently used as a pediatric urgent care facility, while lofts fill its upper four stories.

1915

The General Motors plant of St. Louis, circa 1926. Courtesy Missouri History Museum, St. Louis.

Just one year after he helped organize the General Motors Corporation, W. C. Durant found a man of speed to lead the design team for a new Chevrolet model. Durant was impressed enough to name this new company and its cars after the racer. The skills and colorful personality of Louis Chevrolet had earned him fame as a race car driver in the earliest years of the twentieth century, and a motor he designed powered the Classic Six, a five-passenger touring car that he and a small team built in a loft above a small shop on Grand River Avenue in Detroit. Completed in 1911 after two years of designing, engineering, construction, and testing, this first Chevrolet sold well

enough to dictate creation and expansion. When the 490 model was introduced in 1915, Durant contracted with Russell Gardner, owner of Banner Buggy Company, to assemble Chevrolet cars. Gardner would convert the largest of his buggy sites to build bodies for the Chevrolet 490.

Russell Gardner, a Tennessee native, arrived in St. Louis in 1879 and was building Banner buggies before the turn of the century. Knowing horseless buggies would be the wave of the future, he jumped on the opportunity to partner with Chevrolet in the manufacture and distribution of Chevrolet automobiles for all states west of the Mississippi River. After his sons entered the US Navy during World War I, Gardner sold his business to General Motors, creating the Chevrolet Motor Company of St. Louis in 1918. GM started building a

Chevrolet's light truck assembly plant at 3809 Union Boulevard in 1946. Courtesy Missouri History Museum, St. Louis.

Chevrolet advertising the value of its 1923 Superior Series B. Courtesy National Museum of Transportation Archives.

Chevrolet trucks acting as movable billboard frames in front of the Chevrolet plant, June 1931. Courtesy Missouri History Museum, St. Louis.

new Chevrolet plant at 3809 Union Boulevard, construction of Chevrolet light delivery and one-ton trucks began there in 1920.

When brothers Russell Gardner Junior and Fred Gardner returned from the war, they and their father created the Gardner Motor Company. Already experienced in the assembly rather than manufacture of cars, Gardner chose Lycoming engines throughout its production years and included a four-cylinder Lycoming in its 112-inch wheelbase, mid-priced model introduced in late

A Hilmer Chevrolet dealership Chevrolet truck in front of the Chevrolet plant—a triple Chevy!—in 1931. Courtesy Missouri History Museum, St. Louis.

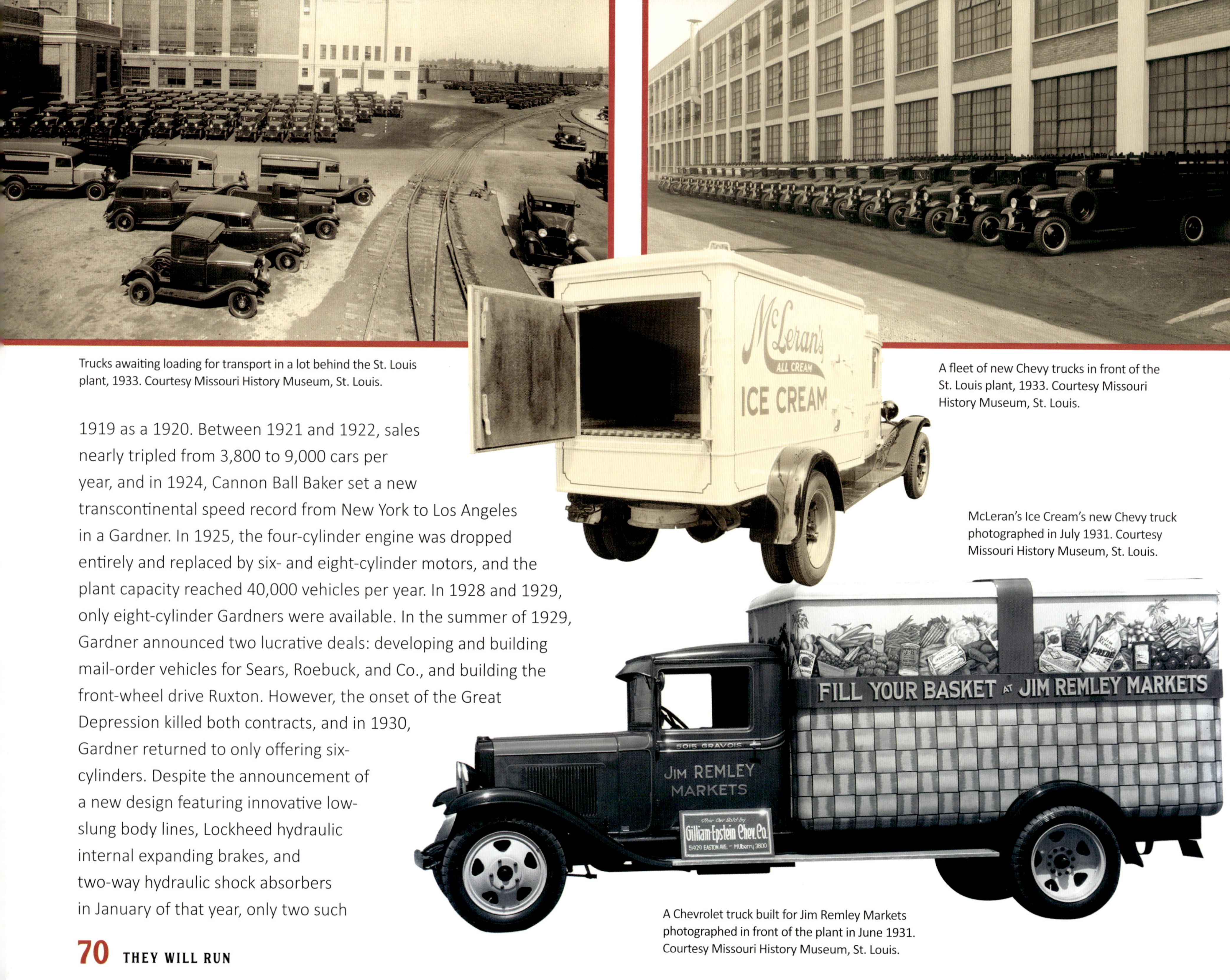

Trucks awaiting loading for transport in a lot behind the St. Louis plant, 1933. Courtesy Missouri History Museum, St. Louis.

A fleet of new Chevy trucks in front of the St. Louis plant, 1933. Courtesy Missouri History Museum, St. Louis.

McLeran's Ice Cream's new Chevy truck photographed in July 1931. Courtesy Missouri History Museum, St. Louis.

A Chevrolet truck built for Jim Remley Markets photographed in front of the plant in June 1931. Courtesy Missouri History Museum, St. Louis.

1919 as a 1920. Between 1921 and 1922, sales nearly tripled from 3,800 to 9,000 cars per year, and in 1924, Cannon Ball Baker set a new transcontinental speed record from New York to Los Angeles in a Gardner. In 1925, the four-cylinder engine was dropped entirely and replaced by six- and eight-cylinder motors, and the plant capacity reached 40,000 vehicles per year. In 1928 and 1929, only eight-cylinder Gardners were available. In the summer of 1929, Gardner announced two lucrative deals: developing and building mail-order vehicles for Sears, Roebuck, and Co., and building the front-wheel drive Ruxton. However, the onset of the Great Depression killed both contracts, and in 1930, Gardner returned to only offering six-cylinders. Despite the announcement of a new design featuring innovative low-slung body lines, Lockheed hydraulic internal expanding brakes, and two-way hydraulic shock absorbers in January of that year, only two such

Vehicle number 10,000,003 to leave the St. Louis
General Motors assembly plant with employees, 1934.
Courtesy Missouri History Museum, St. Louis.

A 1923 Gardner two-door coupe. Courtesy Robert Gardner.

prototypes were built. In mid-1931, Russell Senior received permission from his board of directors to stop building cars, and thereafter, only a few Gardner funeral cars were completed. They would be the last cars built by a St. Louis–based automotive manufacturer.

Less successful was the Bleeck Automobile Company. Incorporated in 1915, John N. and August M. Bleeck intended to build, buy, and sell vehicles from their location at 2914 North Grand Boulevard. Located

in what is now known as the Jeff-Vander-Lou neighborhood, the building still stands, with what appear to have been large showroom windows in front and a garage door along one side. Unfortunately, the building is in poor condition today. It would appear that no vehicles were actually built, and by 1920 the listing for Bleeck Motor Company had disappeared from the St. Louis City Directory. At that time, August Bleeck's occupation was listed simply as "salesman," and when he died in 1933 at the age of 57, his death certificate listed his occupation as a retired delicatessen proprietor.

Gardner Motor Company's innovative one-year warranty, an innovative perk in 1923 when most new vehicle warranties lasted three months or less. Courtesy Robert Gardner.

The D. C. Gilliland Manufacturing and Auto Supply Company was another member of the "Class of 1915" that probably didn't produce any vehicles. *The Horseless Age* reported that David Gilliland, Elmo Omer, and H. and F. Spoeneman had invested $8,000 in a firm created to "manufacture, sell, repair and

A 1923 Gardner. Courtesy Robert Gardner.

A 1929 Gardner phaeton photographed in Guatemala in 1942. Courtesy Robert Gardner.

Grace Genn of Victoria, British Columbia, Canada, photographed in 1931 with her 1929 Gardner coupe. Courtesy Robert Gardner.

A 1931 Gardner Roadster, among the last Gardners built. Courtesy Robert Gardner.

deal in automobiles." According to the 1917 St. Louis City Directory, the firm was located at 4247 Beethoven Avenue. By 1920, the firm was no longer listed among the over 300 automobile repair firms in the directory.

Gardner's Standard Sedan 75 listed for $1,495 in 1928. Courtesy National Museum of Transportation Archives.

Sedan—75
Club Sedan—75 .... $1495
Coupe—75 1395
Victoria—75 1295
Roadster—75 1295
Five-Passenger Touring 1195
Seven-Passenger Touring
Prices upon application
Prices Other Models upon application
(Subject to change)

The Gardner Motor Company, Inc.
St. Louis, Missouri

Gardner Standard Sedan—75

Color .... Two-tone green
Seating ...... Five
Wheelbase .. 122 inches
Wheels ...... Wood
Tires .... 29 x 5.25 inches, balloon
Brakes ...... Foot, expanding on four wheels
Hand, contracting on transmission
Engine ...... Eight cylinder, vertical, cast in block, 2¾ x 4¾ inches; head removable; valves in side; horsepower 24.2, N.A.C.C. rating

Lubrication .. Force feed
Crankshaft .. Five bearing
Radiator .... Cellular
Cooling ..... Water pump
Ignition ..... Storage battery
Starter ...... Two unit
Fuel Feed.... Vacuum
Clutch ...... Dry disc
Speeds ...... Three forward, one reverse
Drive .... Spiral bevel
Rear Springs. Semi-elliptic
Rear Axle.... Semi-floating
Steering ..... Cam and lever

Standard Equipment—Speedometer, ammeter, dash gasoline gauge, electric horn, automatic windshield cleaner, snubbers, stop light, front bumpers, rear view mirror, sun visor, cowl ventilator depressible headlight beams, headlight dimmer, luggage trunk, trunk rack, ventilating windshield, corner lights and dome light.

1917

St. Louis native Theodore C. Brandle, son of Charles and Belle Brandle, taught school from 1910 to 1914, then began working for the Bell Telephone Company, and finally entered the automotive industry in 1915 when he took a job at an automobile repair shop. Later that same year, he founded Westcott Motor Sales Company but changed the company's name to Brandle Motor Company in 1917. Brandle quickly sold it to Chevrolet and became part of the trio of men who founded the Traffic Motor Truck Corporation.

Theodore Brandle and two buddies from work, Guy Wilson, the vice president at Brandle Motor, and Harry Mammen, the general sales manager for the Westcott Motor Car Company of Springfield, Ohio, decided to jump into the truck-building industry with one simple but sturdy offering: the Traffic truck, "the lowest priced 4,000-lb capacity truck in the world." The Traffic Motor Truck Corporation, at its 5200 North Second Street plant, was advertised as featuring "quality production of trucks of one design and one capacity," thereby offering an initial starting price in 1918 of $1,195 for a chassis featuring a six-inch U-channel frame, Red Seal Continental four-cylinder, 239-cubic-inch overhead valve motor, Covert transmission with a Borg and Beck multiple disc clutch, Kingston magneto, Carter carburetor, Timken roller bearings, driver's lazy back, cushioned chair, and a fully painted, varnished, and pinstriped chassis as standard equipment. The retail price of the chassis rose to $1,395 in 1919, $1,495 in 1920, and $1,595 by late 1920, and the company moved to Bosch magnetos. From there, buyers had the option of buying simply the chassis, upgrading to the all-steel dump truck chassis with an all-weather cab and hoist, priced in 1920 at $1,990 complete at the factory, or choosing Traffic cabs and bodies at the dealership.

Though Traffic was quickly able to claim being the "largest exclusive builders of 4,000-lb capacity trucks in the world," it added 1.5- and 3-ton trucks and even offered a 6,000-pound heavy transport truck in 1922. In July of that year, the Traffic Motor Truck Corporation was one of eight automobile, truck, and auto parts manufacturing companies over seven states involved in an $80,000,000 merger to create Associated Motor Industries.[5] The company was headquartered in Dayton, Ohio, but existing plants, including the Traffic plant in St. Louis, continued to manufacture onsite. While the goals of enhanced distribution, maintaining or lowering production and retail costs, and supporting or raising workers' pay were achieved for seven years following the merger, the Great Depression led to the end of Associated Motor Industries and Traffic Motor Trucks in 1929. The former site of the Traffic plant now holds art deco buildings built for the P. D. George Paint Factory in the 1930s.

An ad for the 1920 Traffic Motor Truck.

---

5 The *New York Times*, July 2, 1922

Two St. Louis products working in Washington, DC, in 1925: A 1921 Traffic Motor Truck carrying the new "Orange Whistle Soda" offered by Vess.

By 1917, the Maxwell Brothers were claiming, "Buy once and you'll always buy from the Maxwell Brothers" in national advertising. Located at 3921–3923 Olive Street, Maxwell was proud to be able to offer automotive and truck parts for vehicles built by over fifty manufacturers at discounts of 50% to 80% off their retail price. Their statement, "We are a reliable house—not a small fly-by-night junk man," reflects consumer risks during the period of explosive automotive manufacturing growth.

1919

An ad from Skelton Motors.

On December 1, 1919, the Astra Motors Corporation of St. Louis applied for incorporation with stock valued at $500,000. Hiding behind the creation of that new auto manufacturer, however, was the Associated Motors Corporation of New York City and its goal to overtake the Dorris Motor Car Company. The Astra featured a LeRoi four-cylinder engine on a 108-inch wheelbase and was constructed mostly of purchased parts. Despite its price of $1,318, the Astra could barely outperform a Ford Model T, which cost a fraction as much. George Dorris quickly surmised Associated Motors Corporation's intention, reorganized his company as the Dorris Motors Corporation, bought Astra in late January 1920, and indicated plans were being drawn for a three-story Astra factory adjacent to the Dorris plant. The wily Dorris waited until June of that year to officially end Astra production after only eight to ten Astras were built.

Dr. L. S. Skelton chose a far more direct approach to having an existing company build his cars. The former Vincennes, Indiana, doctor moved to Okmulgee, Oklahoma, in 1893 for health reasons and promptly became an oil man. In 1919, he contracted with the St. Louis Car Company to build 20,000 cars for his Skelton Motors Corporation using Mueck Auto Body bodies built at their two-year-old plant at 4325–4329 West Papin Street in St. Louis. Ed Meissner, president of the St. Louis Car Company, planned to convert fifty existing machines and add 800 workers to build the light four-cylinder, moderately priced Skelton. From 1920 to 1922, the St. Louis Car Company built 1,355 Skeltons, but Dr. Skelton died in 1921, and, for the third time in a span of less than 20 years, the St. Louis Car Company decided to leave the automobile business and focus on its railroad, street, and trolley cars. Mueck Auto Body later moved six miles west to Richmond Heights and converted to the restoration of antique cars. The company remained in the Mueck family and stayed in business until around 1988.

The Scott-Newcomb Motor Carriage

The Standard Engineering Company had been building steam cars for almost three years at its factory at the northwest corner of Eleventh and Olive streets when it decided to incorporate the Standard Steam Corporation and add steam trucks to its offerings in 1920. Its early leaders included notable names, including Russell E. Gardner Jr., two members each of the Bixby and Gratz families, former Packard distributor W. J. Parrish, designer L. L. Scott, and Charles Lemp, the last member of the Lemp brewery family. The company tested its steam-powered car, the "Scott-Newcomb," for almost two years before showing it and claimed it took less than a minute to be operational after lighting a cold boiler by simply turning a switch. The company marketed additional virtues of steam power, including no pressure being placed on the fuel tank, no vaporization of the kerosene or lower-grade oil fuel before burning without odor or smoke, and a single spark plug rather than pilot light for starting its later cars. An entirely enclosed combustion chamber with a forced draft protected the fire from wind, and a lack of gear shifting and other mechanical parts allowed the company to claim their vehicles could travel one thousand miles using just twenty-five gallons of water and without using a fan for cooling purposes. The Fifth Avenue Coach Company of New York City was intrigued enough by the idea of adding steam power within its bus fleet to send its general manager and two of its engineers to inspect and test the Scott-Newcomb system. However, the company only manufactured vehicles through 1921.

Parts Under Hood

An ad for the Scott-Newcomb Auto Steam System offered by the Standard Steam Corporation.

The Stanwood Motor Car Company suffered a similarly short run after incorporating in March of 1920. It used the popular Continental 7R six-cylinder engine in its Stanwood Six, a five-passenger Brewster Green touring car with a 118-inch wheelbase, weight of 2,950 pounds, leather interior, and had a list price of $2,050.[6] A Borg and Beck clutch, Grant-Lees transmission, and Standard Parts rear axle helped the Six reach a top speed of sixty miles per hour. Stanwood's use of parts from other companies rendered its plant an assembly factory rather than a manufacturing line, and the Six was only built for two years.

The 1920 Stanwood Six.

6 *Automobile Trade Journal*, Volume 25, Issues 1–6. Chilton Company, 1920.

ASTRA MOTORS CORPORATION—ST. LOUIS

The ASTRA Car

"The Star of Fours"

Four-cylinder motor cars will always predominate. Even in the present age of Sixes, Eights and Twelves, more than eighty per cent of the motor car production is four-cylinder cars.

The ASTRA is the finality of excellence in Fours. Its design immediately gives it distinction and individuality in the class of high-priced cars, yet the ASTRA will be sold at a popular price.

The power and the unusually light weight of this car, coupled with its precise engineering, its high grade construction and complete equipment insure its economy of operation and its practical freedom from service troubles.

Specifications

Frame—Pressed steel channel section, 6 inches deep, 1½-inch flanges, ⅛-inch thick.

Axles—Front axles are Flint, single-piece drop forging, I-beam section, heat treated, Timken bearings. Rear axles are semi-floating, bevel driving gears, accessible from rear, Timken bearings.

Springs—Semi-elliptic, front 32 inches long, 2 inches wide; rear 46½ inches, 2 inches wide, underslung, chrome vanadium steel.

Motor—Le Roi, 3⅛-inch bore, 4½-inch stroke, L-head, 4-cylinder en bloc, unit power plant.

Carburetor—Zenith.

Gasoline Feed—Vacuum system, 15-gallon tank in rear.

Ignition—Simms high tension magneto.

Lubrication—Splash and piston plunger pump, gravity pressure.

Cooling—Thermo-syphon system, tube and fin type radiator, specially designed for Astra.

Clutch—Borg & Beck, single 8-inch dry plate, control left side and center for domestic cars, right and center for export cars.

Drive—Hotchkiss, 2 universal joints and tubular propeller shaft.

Transmission—Selective sliding gears, 3 speeds forward, 1 reverse, nickel steel gears and shafts.

Steering Gear—Worm and gear, irreversible.

Brakes—Service, external contracting on rear wheels, 12 inches in diameter, 2 inches wide, with equalizer. Internal emergency brakes, expanding on rear wheels, 12 inches in diameter, 1¾ inches wide.

Body—Custom made pressed steel body of exclusive design. Three color options.

Upholstery—Straight piped fitted upholstery of genuine buffed black leather, Marshall springs.

Wheels—Wire wheels of newest type.

Wheel Base—107¼ inches.

Equipment—Westinghouse two-unit lighting and starting system. Astra one-man top with top cover and quick adjustable interior fastening side curtains with plate glass light in rear of car. Astra rain vision and ventilating and rain-proof windshield, speedometer, motor driven horn, headlights with auxiliary bulbs, dash and tail light lamp, robe carrier, foot rail, cigar lighter, inspection light, pump, jack, tool kit, tire repair outfit, special tire carrier at rear, ignition lock.

Tires—31" x 4".

Weight—2,000 lbs.

Ready for Delivery July 1, 1920.

An advertisement for the 1920 Astra extolling its four-cylinder motor. Courtesy National Museum of Transportation Archives.

This 1917 Astra demonstrates the unusual and possibly unappealing shapes that helped convince George Dorris he wanted no part of building them after buying the company. Courtesy Dorris Family Collection.

1921

Herbert Scheel took an inventive road when he created the Scheel Motors Company for the manufacture and sale of a rotary valve, four-cylinder engine he designed, claiming it developed in excess of eighty horsepower. The Scheel rotary made an impressive debut on dirt tracks in 1921, and in early 1923, Scheel partnered with Louis Chevrolet of Indianapolis to build race cars for the Detroit-based Frontenac Motor Company race team for the Indianapolis 500 using his rotary engine.

At least one car was completed, but after it ran a few practice laps, its roller bearings failed, it was immediately put away, and the entry of four Chevrolet-Scheel cars was withdrawn. In December 1923, Scheel signed a contract with a syndicate of car builders on the East Coast, led by Arthur Sinclair, to provide motors for the proposed Sinclair race cars, but no Sinclair cars with Scheel motors were built. To avoid angry stockholders, Scheel disappeared somewhere in Texas.

Unlike Scheel Motors, Luedinghaus Truck was looking for neither speed in vehicles nor the early demise of its company. German natives Henry and Louis Espenscheid opened a blacksmith shop in St. Louis in 1843 and quickly added carriage and wagon building to their shop. The L. Espenschied Wagon Company equipped Mormons heading west in 1853 with fourteen wagons and had a large contract to supply the Union army during the Civil War with wagons and wheels. In 1880, Luedinghaus

Left: An example of the Scheel rotary valve head engine. Courtesy Museum of American Speed.
Right: The Museum of American Speed's cutaway of a Scheel rotary valve head engine showcases the rotary valve.

The Hill-Behan Lumber Company 's Luedinghaus lumber truck still survives at the National Museum of Transportation. Courtesy National Museum of Transportation Archives.

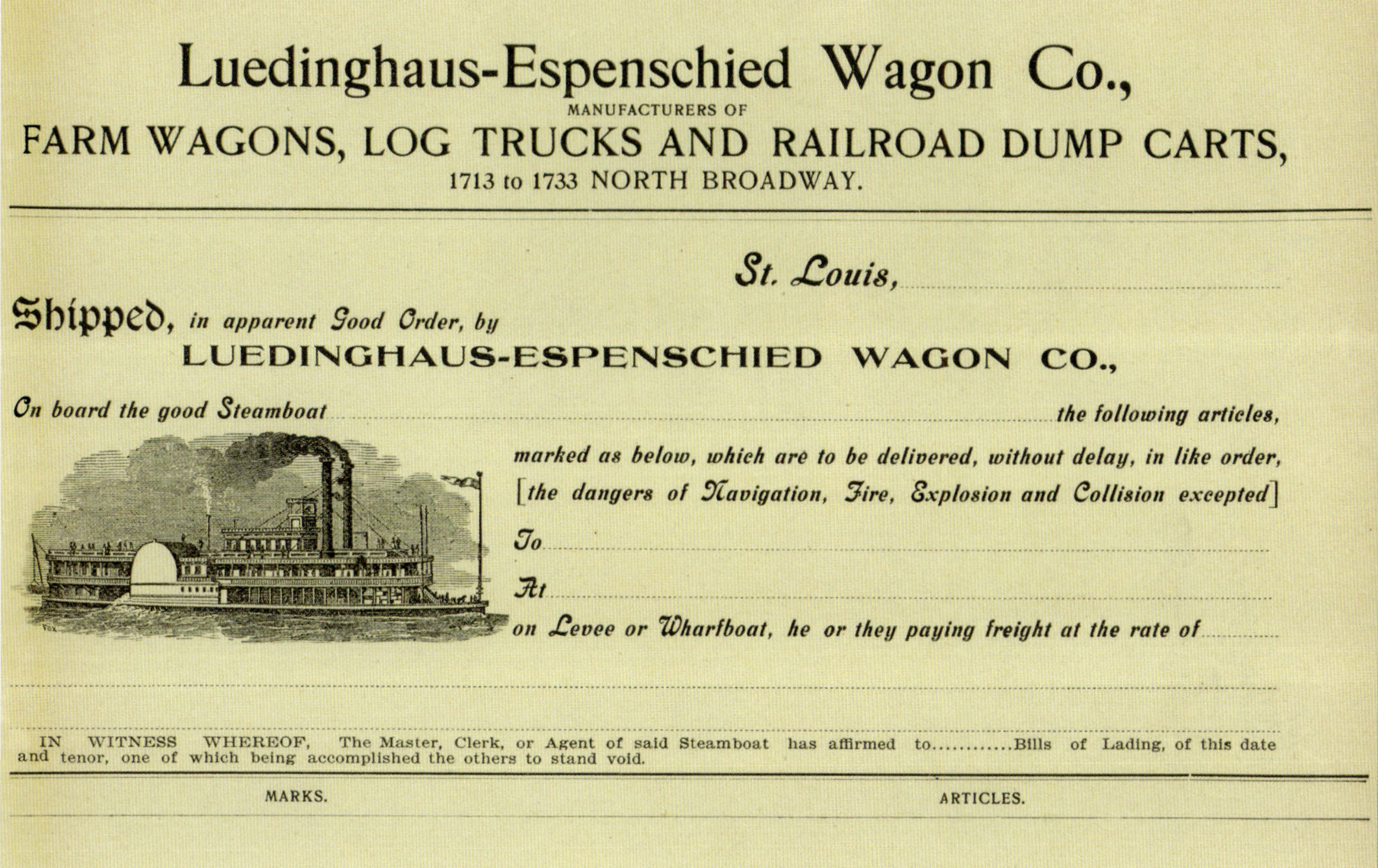

A bill of lading form offered by the Luedinghaus & Espenschied Wagon Company. Courtesy Missouri History Museum, St. Louis.

combined with another freight and commercial wagon builder, the Arensmann-Luedinghaus Wagon Manufacturing Company, to create the Luedinghaus & Espenschied Wagon Company. In the 1920s, the company added the building of motor trucks, truck bodies, and trailers to its wagon building and remained in business until the 1930s.

The automotive builders based in St. Louis were not immune to the Great Depression. Beginning with the crash of the stock market in October 1929, the Depression led to such high unemployment, massive deflation, and loss of gross domestic product that automobile purchases plunged for over a decade. None of the automobile manufacturers born in St. Louis survived the Depression. Just as economic numbers began to return to stability by 1939, and as the fields of the plains recovered from years of drought in the mid-1930s that had not just compromised the ability of farmers to buy vehicles but the vocation of agriculture itself, something else arose to force the car builders to change lanes—World War II.

1926

St. Louis has been home to a number of builders of apparatus for fire trucks. In 1918, the General Manufacturing Corporation of St. Louis began building fire extinguishers, and by the time the company moved to 4127-4133 Forest Park Avenue in 1926, the company's principal product was motor-driven fire apparatus for installation on commercial truck chassis. Ten years later, the company moved to Detroit. During its time in St. Louis, it built a Monarch model for the Kirkwood Fire Department and delivered it in September, 1932. Featuring a Hercules six-cylinder engine, the truck was acquired by the Antique Warehouse in 2002 and restored to operation. Courtesy Greg R. Rhomberg, Antique Warehouse.

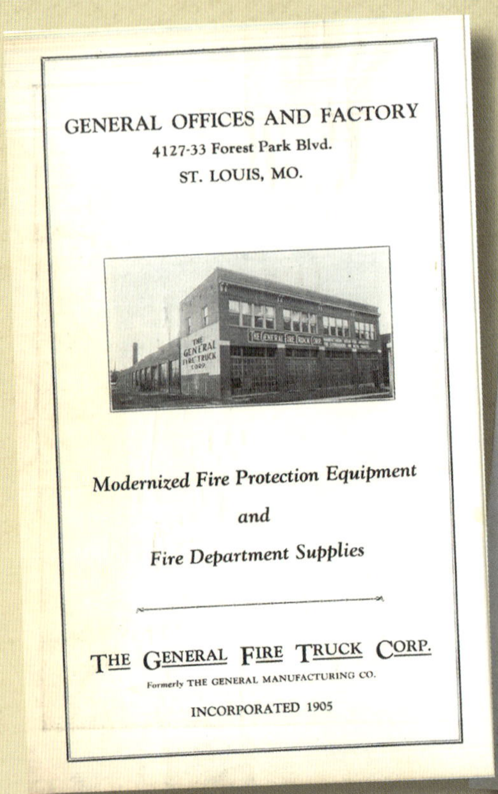

GENERAL OFFICES AND FACTORY

4127-33 Forest Park Blvd.
ST. LOUIS, MO.

Modernized Fire Protection Equipment

and

Fire Department Supplies

THE GENERAL FIRE TRUCK CORP.

Formerly THE GENERAL MANUFACTURING CO.

INCORPORATED 1905

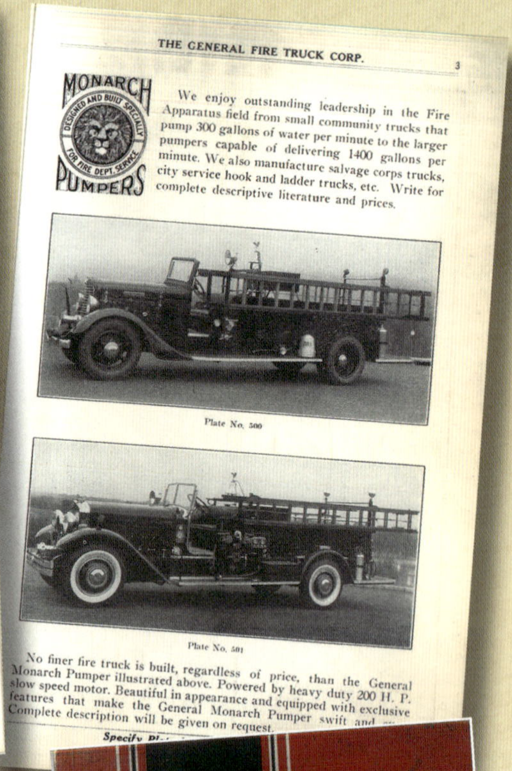

THE GENERAL FIRE TRUCK CORP.

MONARCH PUMPERS

We enjoy outstanding leadership in the Fire Apparatus field from small community trucks that pump 300 gallons of water per minute to the larger pumpers capable of delivering 1400 gallons per minute. We also manufacture salvage corps trucks, city service hook and ladder trucks, etc. Write for complete descriptive literature and prices.

Plate No. 500

Plate No. 501

No finer fire truck is built, regardless of price, than the General Monarch Pumper illustrated above. Powered by heavy duty 200 H. P. slow speed motor. Beautiful in appearance and equipped with exclusive features that make the General Monarch Pumper swift and sure. Complete description will be given on request.

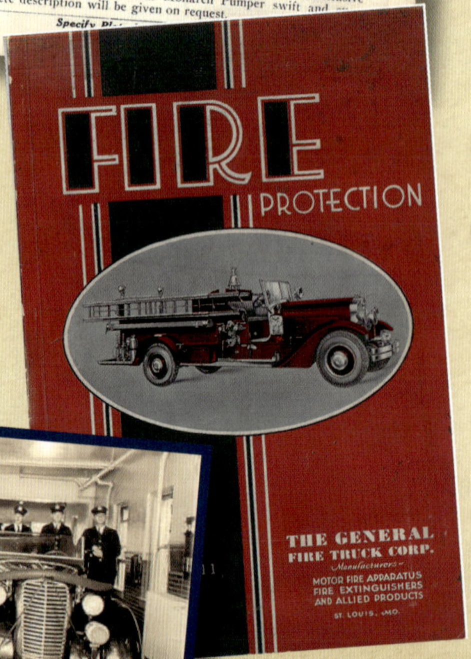

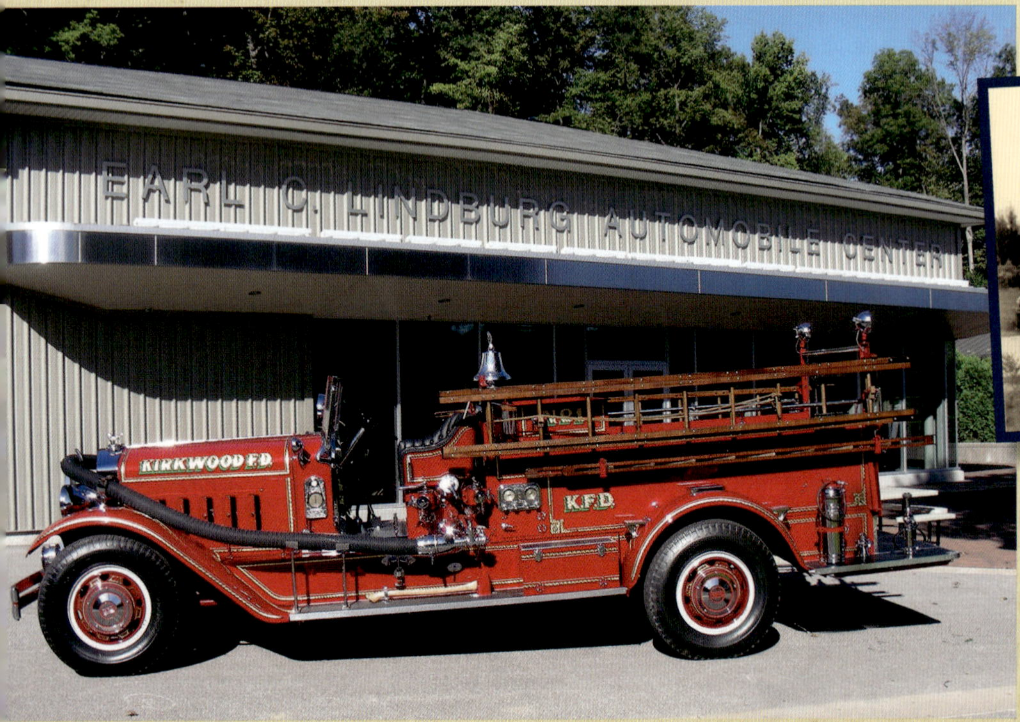

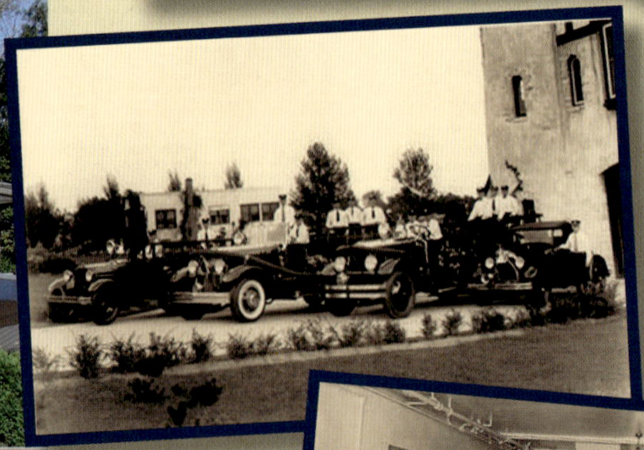

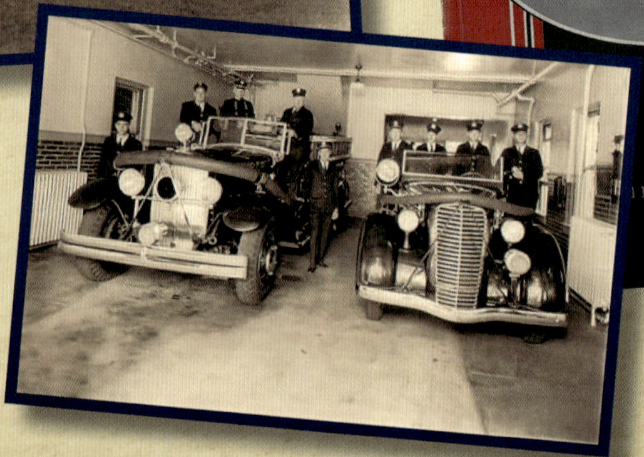

St. Louis
BUILT RIGHT HERE IN ST. LOUIS!
Beautiful....Modern
...GENERAL MONARCH PUMPERS
Powered by heavy duty, low speed 200 H. P. motors and equipped with automatic pump throw-out clutch, noiseless transmission, built-in winter-front shutters, silent pump and exhaust....all exclusive features and found only in the magnificent GENERAL MONARCH FIRE TRUCK.
When thinking about a Fire Truck for your city or community, let us figure with you, whether you need a pumper with capacity of 300 or 1400 gallons per minute.
"DUAL GRIP"
SAFETY
FIRE HOSE COUPLING
FLAT CURED CONSTRUCT
GENERAL
MUNICIPAL FIRE
In Use in 90% of the
and Towns in Mi
THE GEN
ESTABLISHED 1905
KIRKWOOD F.D.
K.F.D.
MANUFACTURERS MOTOR FIRE APPARAT
FIRE EXTINGUISHERS AND METAL
THE GENERAL MANUFACTU

The Pope-Hartford Motor Car Company chose Delmar Boulevard for its St. Louis home in 1910. Courtesy Missouri History Museum, St. Louis.

Chapter Four

BRINGING THE VEHICLE TO THE PEOPLE

Delmar, Locust, and South Kingshighway Automobile Rows

Many cities lay claim to having an "Automobile Row" at some point in their history. Kansas City, for example, had a full-fledged automobile district centered around Eighteenth and McGee by the mid-1920s. St. Louis, however, may be the only city to boast three distinct Automobile Rows at various points in time. When the Pope-Hartford Motor Company of Hartford, Connecticut, decided to open an accessory and parts retail store at 5887–89 Delmar in St. Louis in 1910, it also unknowingly opened Delmar Boulevard as one of the city's two early "automobile rows" lined with companies selling, servicing, and providing materials to maintain and accessorize automobiles.

With its streetcar service along the city's burgeoning east–west corridor, convenience to the Midtown area with shopping and entertainment that rivaled offerings downtown, and location three miles west of another "automobile row" on Locust Street at a time when city residents were beginning to move west, Delmar Boulevard became the home of forty-nine automobile-related dealerships, shops, and stores by 1921. As referenced in the National Register of Historic Places nomination for the Roberts Chevrolet dealership, which moved into the Pope-Hartford building in 1935, the number and variety of shops on the street in 1921 were significant:

NAME OF BUSINESS	ADDRESS	TYPE OF BUSINESS
Art B. Mooney Tire Company	4547 Delmar	Tires
Auto Electric Service Company	5090 Delmar	Repair
Baldorf Tire Company	5866 Delmar	Tires
Becker & Schuller Auto Repair Company	4501 Delmar	Repair
Bray-Hambuechen Motor Company	5127–5135 Delmar	Dealership
Clardel Garage	5635 Delmar	Garage
Continental Auto Supply Company	5837 Delmar	Supplies
Day-N-Nite Auto Repair Company	4738 Delmar	Repair
Delmar Academy Garage Sales Corp.	5090 Delmar	Dealership/Garage
Delmar Auto Repair Company	4738 Delmar	Repair
Delmar Automobile Company	4943 Delmar	Dealership
Delmar Motor Car Company	5875 Delmar	Garage
Delmar-Union Garage	5263 Delmar	Garage
Delway Auto Repair Company	5037 Delmar	Repair
Downs Auto Company	5883 Delmar	Dealership
E. B. Whitworth Motor Sales Company	5080 Delmar	Dealership
Edward Martin	5841 Delmar	Repair
Flint Motor Car Company	4710 Delmar	Dealership
Gabriel Johnston	6153 Delmar	Garage
Gates Auto Laundry & Supply Company	5760 Delmar	Supplies
Gill-Foote & Company Battery Service	5243 Delmar	Supplies
Goodfellow Garage-Auto Repair Company	5804–06 Delmar	Garage
H. H. Miller Tire Company	6172 Delmar	Tires

NAME OF BUSINESS	ADDRESS	TYPE OF BUSINESS
Haines Auto Radiator Company	4624 Delmar	Auto Parts
Hamilton Garage	5837 Delmar	Garage
Harrigan & Toebe	4151 Delmar	Repair
Heinrich Automobile Company	5123 Delmar	Dealership/Repair
Horn Electric Auto Company	4601 Delmar	Repair
Horras Piston Ring Company	5012 Delmar	Supplies
Hudson-Frampton Motor Car Company	4525–37 Delmar	Dealership
J. Henry Brinkoetter	4541 Delmar	Auto Painter
LaGrave Automobile Repair Company	5158 Delmar	Repair
Lasker Motor Company	5143 Delmar	Dealership
Maurice Stiffelman	4969 Delmar	Tires
McNiece-Hill Motor Company	5187–89 Delmar	Dealership/Repair/Supplies/Tires
Metropolitan Auto Repair Company	4468 Delmar	Repair
Milbur Motor Mart	5883 Delmar	Repair
O. Kasten & Company	4618 Delmar	Repair
Phillips Automobile Company	5053 Delmar	Dealership
Revell & Jaco Auto Repair Company	6153 Delmar	Repair
Riehl Battery Service	5263 Delmar	Supplies
Roger Putnamr	5711 Delmar	Tires
Tiger Tire Company	4626 Delmar	Tires
University Garage	6131/6020 Delmar	Garage
Vesper Buick Auto Company	5023 Delmar	Dealership
Welling Motor Company	5033 Delmar	Dealership/Trucks
West End Battery Service	5845 Delmar	Supplies
William H. Lofland	3725 Delmar	Dealership
William Young Carriage Company	4524 Delmar	Auto Painter/Upholsterer
Walsh Motor Car Company	4919–23, 5127–5135 Delmar	Dealership
West Side Buick Company	5023–29 Delmar	Dealership
White Auto Repair Company	4728 Delmar	Repair

Delmar

Delmar remained an important site of automobile sales and service for a half-century after Pope-Hartford moved there in 1910. In fact, in that building alone, a total of nineteen automobile-related companies were located before 1959. However, westward and southward migrations of residents in the area began during the Great Depression, accelerated in the postwar years, and, as the businesses followed the residents, rendered many storefronts and garages along Delmar Boulevard vacant by the early 1960s.

This former filling station at 5162 Delmar has served as a restaurant in its second career.

An almost-new 1907 Maxwell is photographed in front of its home dealership, the Peper Automobile Company, at 4921 Delmar in 1908. The A. H. Sullivan & Company repair shop moved from Laclede Avenue to 4527-4529 Delmar in 1915. Courtesy Missouri History Museum, St. Louis.

Delmar Motors at 4525 Delmar Boulevard showcasing trucks early in 1935.
© *St. Louis Post-Dispatch* and courtesy Missouri History Museum, St. Louis.
Sievers, Isaac, 1886–1954

The Hudson & Terraplane Sales dealership's parts
department at 4535 Delmar in October 1935.
© Hudson & Terraplane Sales Corporation and
courtesy Missouri History Museum, St. Louis., Sievers,
Isaac, 1886–1954

Display advertising the Hudson car radio at
the Hudson & Terraplane Sales Corporation,
4535 Delmar Boulevard, in 1937. © Hudson
& Terraplane Sales Corporation and courtesy
Missouri History Museum, St. Louis.

A large group of automobile dealers gathered in front of the Hudson-Frampton dealership at 4525 Delmar Boulevard in November 1934. © *St. Louis Post-Dispatch* and courtesy Missouri History Museum, St. Louis., Sievers, Isaac, 1886–1954

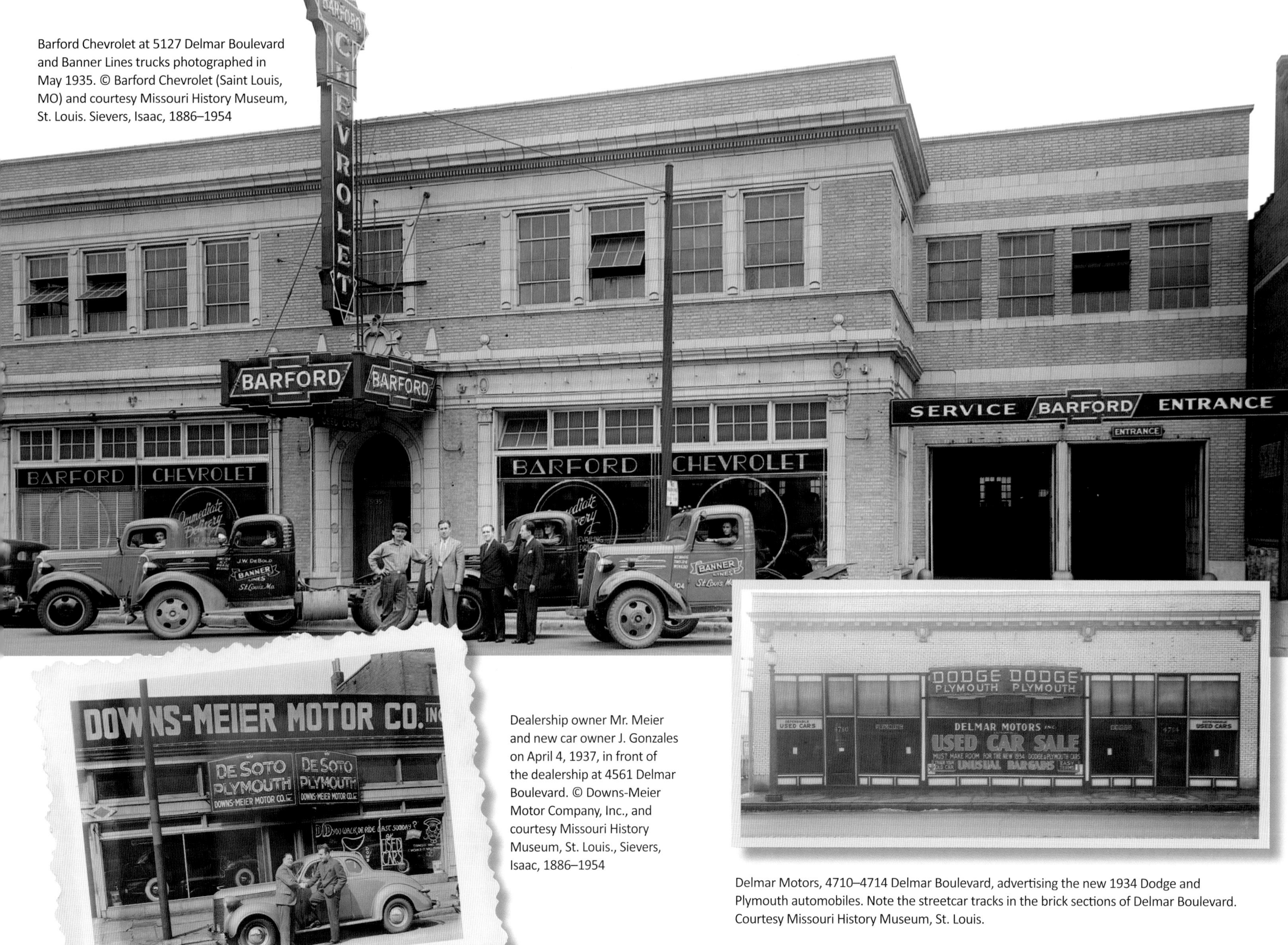

Barford Chevrolet at 5127 Delmar Boulevard and Banner Lines trucks photographed in May 1935. © Barford Chevrolet (Saint Louis, MO) and courtesy Missouri History Museum, St. Louis. Sievers, Isaac, 1886–1954

Dealership owner Mr. Meier and new car owner J. Gonzales on April 4, 1937, in front of the dealership at 4561 Delmar Boulevard. © Downs-Meier Motor Company, Inc., and courtesy Missouri History Museum, St. Louis., Sievers, Isaac, 1886–1954

Delmar Motors, 4710–4714 Delmar Boulevard, advertising the new 1934 Dodge and Plymouth automobiles. Note the streetcar tracks in the brick sections of Delmar Boulevard. Courtesy Missouri History Museum, St. Louis.

The Lasker Motor Company was located at 5143 Delmar.

The McNiece-Hill Motor Company sold Lincolns from its new building at 5187–89 Delmar beginning in 1920.

Legends were caught standing side-by-side in this 1922 portrait taken in the Lincoln room of the Lincoln Motor Company. Henry Ford of Ford Motor Company and assembly line fame stands alongside Henry Leland, founder of Cadillac and Lincoln while Edsel Ford holds a quill pen, about to sign a document, and Wilfred Leland sits alongside him. Portraits of Abraham Lincoln hang on wall in background. Courtesy Detroit Public Library.

An artist, likely hired by Durant to help market the Muncie, Indiana, auto manufacturer's cars, drew a 1922 Durant B-22 car. Printed on front: "Durant. Six cylinder four passenger coupe, model B-22, $2250, f.o.b. Muncie, Ind." Handwritten on the back of the image is "Durant, 1922." Courtesy Detroit Public Library.

A 1937 view of the Clay Goodloe Auto Company at 5841 Delmar Boulevard. © *St. Louis Post-Dispatch* and courtesy Missouri History Museum, St. Louis.

The Delmar-Union Garage and Riehl Battery were located at 5261–5263 Delmar.

Right: The Phillips Automobile Company opened its showroom at 5053 Delmar in 1909.

A photo of the intersection of Delmar and Union taken in the early 1930s by St. Louis City's Department of Streets and Sewers' photographic division. Meissler Drug, on the opposite corner of the Delmar-Union Garage, is shown. Courtesy Missouri History Museum, St. Louis.

Locust

St. Louis's other early Automobile Row was located in midtown. While one of the earliest businesses in that location—the Hurck Motor and Cycle Company—opened at 2113 Olive in 1904 and stayed until 1951, the locus of automobile sales and services was one street over, Locust Street, from the teens to the beginning of World War II. Below we take a tour of this area and consider the glorious buildings that still stand.

1815 LOCUST

As earlier horse-powered American wheels often moved west from an eastern starting point, a good point from which to begin a drive down St. Louis's preeminent "Automobile Row" is at the former home of the Weber Implement and Automobile Company. Designed by noted St. Louis architect Preston Bradshaw, a favorite among automobile-related company owners, the building was completed in 1919 and housed auto dealerships and distributors for its first twenty years. It later hosted a number of radio and vinyl record suppliers.

Mound City Motors, 1821 Locust Street, in 1932. © Weber Implement and Automobile Company and courtesy Missouri History Museum, St. Louis., Sievers, Isaac, 1886–1954

Three unidentified men posing next to a 1934 DeSoto Airflow in front of Mound City Motors. © Weber Implement and Automobile Company and courtesy Missouri History Museum, St. Louis.

The Weber Implement and Automobile Company building and used car lot at 18th Street and Locust Street, photographed in July 1937. © Weber Implement and Automobile Company and courtesy Missouri History Museum, St. Louis.

Chassis of a 1932 Plymouth displayed on the showroom floor at the Weber Implement and Automobile Company at 1821–1827 Locust. © Weber Implement and Automobile Company and courtesy Missouri History Museum, St. Louis.

1900 LOCUST

Built in 1897, this building has housed everything from an early Hupmobile dealership to a restaurant owned by a popular player for the St. Louis Cardinals.

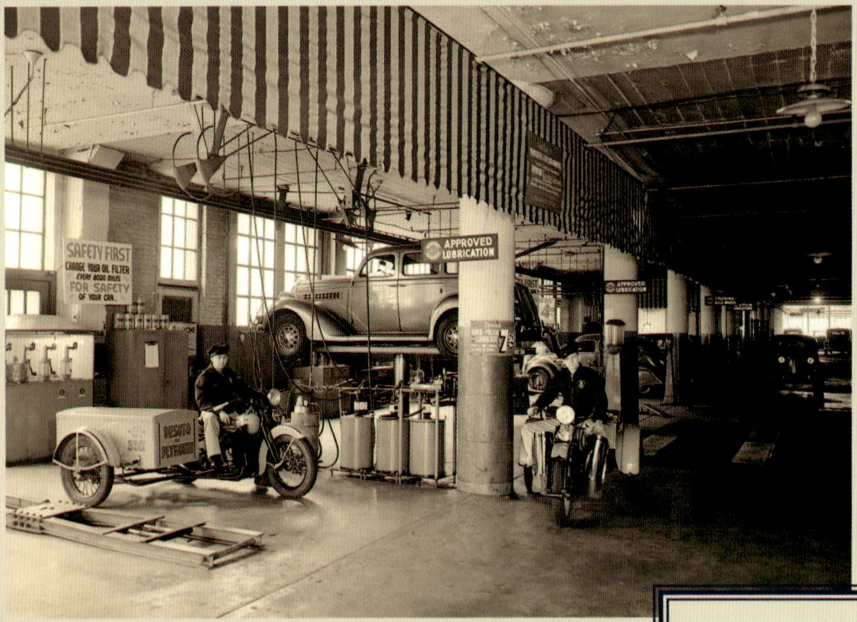

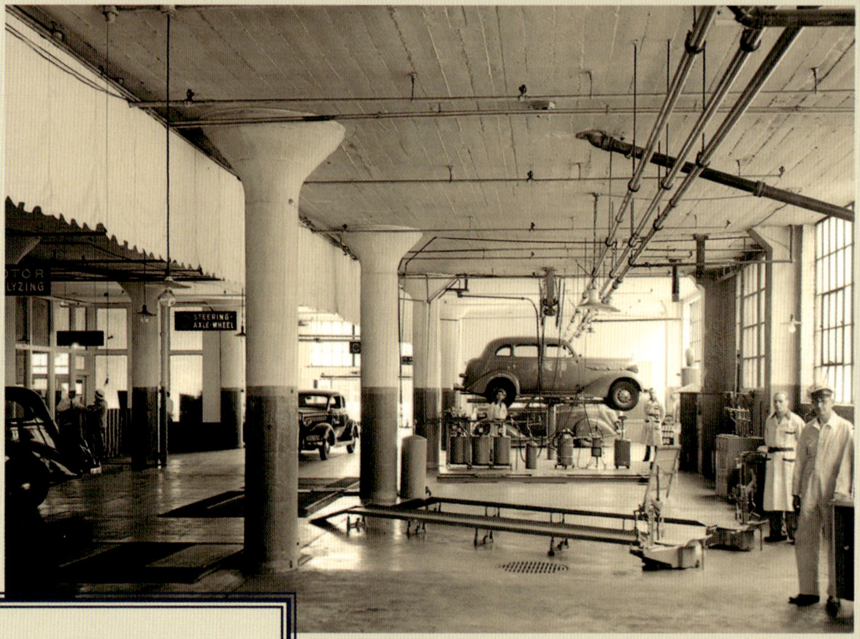

MOUND CITY MOTORS
19TH AND LOCUST

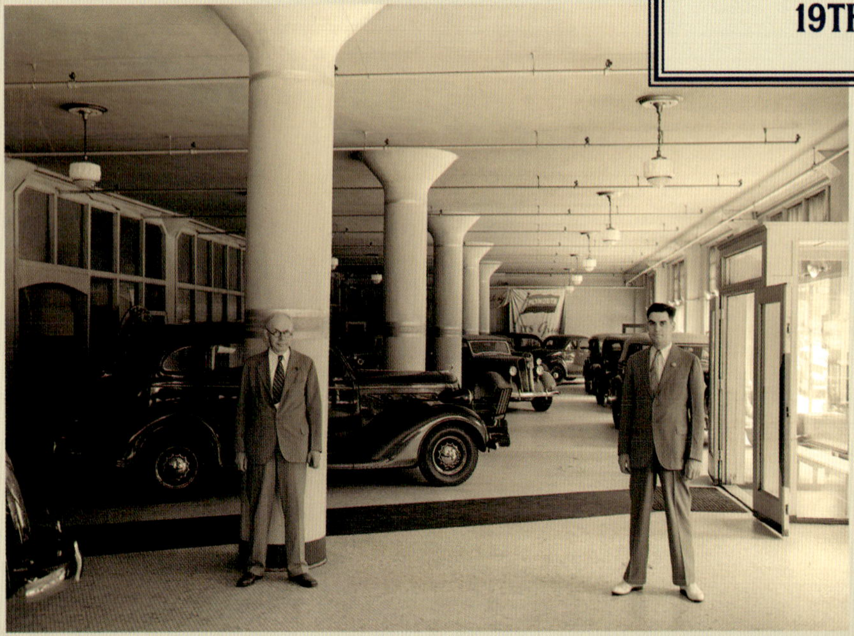

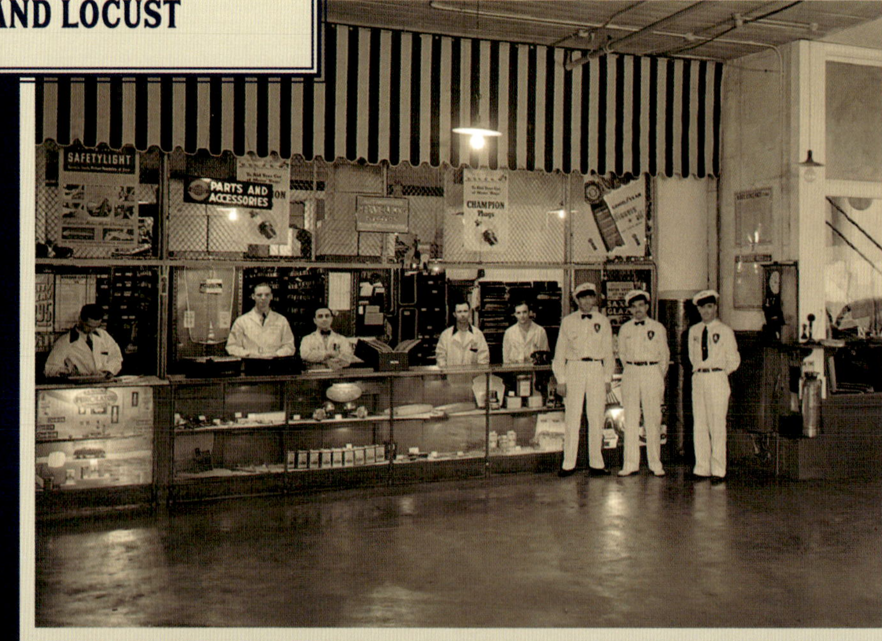

All photos © Chrysler Corporation and courtesy Missouri History Museum, St. Louis:, Sievers, Isaac, 1886–1954

An exhibit of DeSotos inside the Weber Implement Company photographed during the summer of 1934. © Weber Implement and Automobile Company and courtesy Missouri History Museum, St. Louis, Sievers Studio

Emil Weber posing with a car outside of a Weber Implement and Automobile Company showroom in the 1900 block of Locust Street in April of 1931. © Weber Implement and Automobile Company and courtesy Missouri History Museum, St. Louis., Sievers, Isaac, 1886–1954.

The employees of Automotive Electrical Service posed in front of the company's building at 2131 Locust Street at an unknown date but likely in the late 1920s before the stock market crash in October 1929. Courtesy Missouri History Museum, St. Louis.

Mound City Motors at 1821 Locust Street in the summer of 1931. © Weber Implement, Sievers, Isaac, 1886–1954

Mound City Motors at 19th and Locust in 1936. © Sidney Weber, Inc., and courtesy Missouri History Museum, St. Louis., Sievers, Isaac, 1886–1954

A 1932 photograph of the large and versatile building. © Weber Implement and Automobile Company at 1829 Locust Street. Courtesy Missouri History Museum, St. Louis., Sievers, Isaac, 1886–1954

The Weber Motor Car Company knew a building with distinctive lines and details would be a great base from which to sell Studebakers, well known for their own unique looks.

The Sidney Weber, Inc. building at 2217 Locust Street in 1936. © Sidney Weber, Inc., and courtesy Missouri History Museum, St. Louis., Sievers, Isaac, 1886–1954

The former Packard Motors dealership at 2201 Locust Street up for sale in 1954. © Holder unknown, courtesy Missouri History Museum, St. Louis., Dorrill Studio.

2201 LOCUST

Packards meant style, luxury, and prestige—qualities happily marketed by an investor adaptively reusing a former Packard dealership as luxury lofts.

The showroom of the Packard-Missouri Motor Company at 2201 Locust, photographed here circa 1916, exemplifies the high standards twhich Packard's customers expected its vehicles to meet. In that era, if a driver wanted the best, he or she bought one of the three "Ps"—Packard, Peerless, or Pierce-Arrow. © W. C. Persons, courtesy Missouri History Museum, St. Louis.

The quiet elegance and strength conveyed by the architecture of the Packard-Missouri Motor Company's showroom on Locust in 1916 echoed the automobiles housed and marketed within it. © W. C. Persons, courtesy Missouri History Museum, St. Louis.

2223–2227 LOCUST

Samuel L. Haas didn't only know hats . . . although Samuel L. Haas had this building built in 1923 and used its upper floors for the manufacture and sale of hats, he knew marketing as well as haberdashery. Recognizing the draw of Automobile Row, he leased the first floor of the Haas Building to automobile dealerships for the display and sale of their cars. Many of those buyers headed upstairs to shop for new hats to wear in their new car.

A fleet of Oldsmobiles parked in front of Olds Motor Works, 2223 Locust Street, in 1931. © Olds Motor Works (Saint Louis, MO) and courtesy Missouri History Museum, St. Louis., Meyers, Ed.

2309 LOCUST

The Auburn Graves Motor Company used this distinctive 1914 tan brick building as its dealership.

2315–2327 LOCUST

Shortly after J. H. Phillips had a two-story dealership building built at 2315 Locust in 1914, he began offering a guarantee for new Hudsons bought from his dealership—a novelty for Hudson itself and an appealing way to sell cars. When buyers of new Hudsons from the dealership brought the cars back for monthly inspections, the Hudson-Phillips Motor Car Company would offer free service for one year after the car was purchased. However, Phillips only utilized the building for two years before selling it to Mendenhall Ford, which used it from 1916 to 1950. Mendenhall added a matching four-story addition on the building's west side at 2321 Locust in 1924, although for three years during the Great Depression, it used only the original one-story section. For one of those years—1936—stylish and speedy Auburns were sold from the ground floor of the western building, but Auburn and its sisters, Cord and Duesenberg, went out of business the following year. Mendenhall then sold and serviced Fords in the buildings until 1950.

Two who know power and style—Italian boxer Primo Carnera and an Auburn—photographed in front of the Mendenhall Ford building in 1936, the one year Auburns were included in the dealership's offerings, the last year they were made, and two years after Carnera lost his world heavyweight title. © Auburn Graves Motor Company and courtesy Missouri History Museum, St. Louis.

Top: Renowned St. Louis photographer Isaac Sievers knew a 1936 Cord had the shapes worthy of a good shot on Locust Street's Automobile Row. © *St. Louis Star-Times* and courtesy Missouri History Museum, St. Louis.

Bottom: Mendenhall Motors at 2323 Locust Street in early 1935. © *St. Louis Post-Dispatch* and courtesy Missouri History Museum, St. Louis., Sievers, Isaac, 1886–1954

2700 LOCUST

The Delhi Battery & Supply Company must have already been profitable in this building in 1921, as they had three Ford Model Ts registered to this address with the city that year.

2801 LOCUST

Sales of Oaklands and Pontiacs had gone so well for the Mississippi Valley Motor Company at its original 3137 Locust showroom location that, eight years after opening it in 1916, the company had built and moved to its new building at 2801 Locust. The height of the four-story building, completed in 1924, allowed the dealership to prominently advertise "Oakland" in paint. The building now serves as a wedding venue.

In a 2017 auction, this McQuay-Norris tin parts bin from the 1930s sold for over $600, and the sign sold for almost $3000. Courtesy Barrett-Jackson.

2806–2812 LOCUST

Known for the engineering and quality of its automotive parts and its knowledgeable young engineers who traveled the country in its teardrop cars—and tore down and rebuilt them for parts retailers—the McQuay-Norris Manufacturing Company first built and opened on Locust at 2808 in 1914. One year later, it added an additional connected building at 2806 Locust, which gave the company an open second floor for parts inventory.

2814 LOCUST

The animals are running amuck on Locust's Automobile Row . . . at least on the front of the Cole Motor Company's building, finished in 1914 at 2814 Locust. Incorporated in Missouri to sell Cole automobiles, the company quickly joined forces with noted early St. Louis motor car businessman E. W. Arbogast, who was selling Monroe and American vehicles down the street at 3116 Locust.

Close-up view of Indiana native and driver "Farmer Bill" Endicott posing in a Cole 30 racecar. Printed on front: "Bill Endicott in Cole 30." Handwritten on back: "Cole." Endicott was inducted into the National Racing Hall of Fame in June 2019. Courtesy Detroit Public Library.

2920–2922 LOCUST

Dating to 1916, the Cadillac Building was home to several automobile-related firms during the prewar period. The Cadillac Automobile Company of St. Louis was there until its move to larger facilities down the street in 1919. The next automotive tenant was the Orthwein Motor Corporation in 1920, followed by the Tilton-Gardner Motor Company (1926), the Lurie Motor Car Company (1928), the Jordan–St. Louis Company (1930), the Archer Mann Motor Company (1932), the Southwest Willys Company (1933), and the Guaranty Motor Corporation (1935). A series of non-automotive tenants followed, and the building was placed on the National Register of Historic Places in 2005.

The Spanish Revival stucco building at 2921 Locust Street during its Wilson Motor Car Company days, in which Haynes, Elgin, Harroun and Acason Trucks were sold from its store front while Whistle Bottle Works was operating in the back. Courtesy Missouri History Museum, St. Louis.

2924 LOCUST

Although it didn't need the building façade ornamentation often seen on early automotive dealerships, the McGuire National Lubricating Oil and Supply company got it when they hired Stephens & Pearson as the architects for its store at 2924 Locust. Opened in 1914, this early figure on Locust's Automobile Row set an eye-catching standard with terra cotta, glazed bricks, and a large display window to attract customers.

Oil engineer testing motor oil. Courtesy Detroit Public Library.

The Wildgen-Vincel Oldsmobile dealership at 2927 Locust Street in 1927. © Wildgen-Vincel, Inc., and courtesy Missouri History Museum, St. Louis.

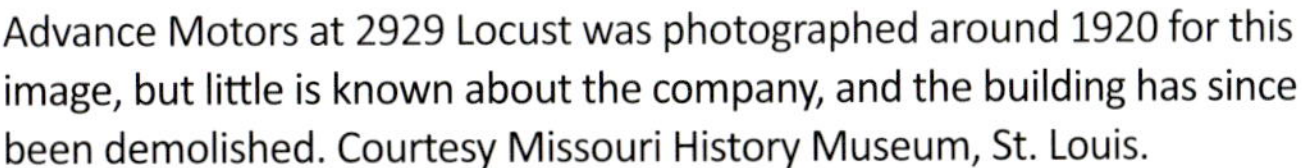

Advance Motors at 2929 Locust was photographed around 1920 for this image, but little is known about the company, and the building has since been demolished. Courtesy Missouri History Museum, St. Louis.

2926–2036 LOCUST

According to the plaque placed on the Cole-Standard Building by the Horseless Carriage Club of Missouri, this was the site of no fewer than ten (!) automobile dealerships between 1919 and 1935. Designed by renowned architect Preston Bradshaw, the building at various times served as a dealership for Standard Eight automobiles, Cole vehicles, Holmes automobiles, Stephens cars, and the used-car operation of G. M. Berry. Wildgen-Vincel Oldsmobile sold used cars there from 1932 to 1935. And, according to its National Register of Historic Places filing, the final automotive business there was the Guaranty Motor Corporation, which was replaced by the Barrett Electrical Supply Company from 1940 through the 1960s. Today the building is home to the Nu-Art Series Gallery.

3000 LOCUST

Built in 1920 and designed by Preston Bradshaw, the Nash St. Louis Motor Company/Southwest Nash Motor Company Building housed both wholesale and retail operations of the Nash St. Louis Motor Company for approximately a decade. The Southwest Willys Company was there until 1935, after which the building housed a variety of nonautomotive organizations. As of this publication date, the building is vacant and for sale.

The dealership building for the Southwest Willys Company at the corner of Garrison and Locust hints Willys don't need plain roads. © *St. Louis Post-Dispatch* and courtesy Missouri History Museum, St. Louis. Sievers, Isaac, 1886–1954

The 1918 Nash was the first designed by George Nash. Courtesy Detroit Public Library.

3001 LOCUST

The Diamond Rubber Company outgrew its original location at 3965 Olive Street and had this building, with its incredibly detailed cornice, built in 1913, making it one of the early auto-related companies on Locust. Another tire store, B. F. Goodrich Rubber Company, followed Diamond, as did several dealerships and parts suppliers. The building was used for storage starting in the 1960s and now houses a restaurant.

1911 Amplex. Courtesy Detroit Public Library.

3005–3007 LOCUST

The Missouri Motor Car Company opened its first showroom at 1131 Olive in 1910 with the goal of selling higher-end vehicles such as the Amplex, Marmon, and Simplex. The firm apparently catered to an upscale buyer; the 1913 Marmon Six was advertised at a price of $5,000 (approximately $128,000 today!). In early 1912, the firm began building a striking new showroom that blended Greek revival shapes with white glazed blocks and Prairie lines at 3005–3007 Locust. Coincidentally, a planning, architectural, and design firm currently occupies it.

The Goodyear Tire and Rubber Company's store and shop at 3010–12 Locust Street was both strategically placed toward the western end of automobile row and elegantly designed in an attempt to help it stand out among the many tire shops on Locust. © W. C. Persons, courtesy Missouri History Museum, St. Louis.

3015 LOCUST

Built in 1916, the Franklin Building housed the Franklin Auto Supply Company, a distributor of the Franklin automobile. Franklins had a somewhat unusual air-cooled engine and were handsome machines. As with so many others, however, the Franklin succumbed to the Great Depression. And, like many other buildings on Automobile Row, the Franklin Building went through a series of tenants, seemingly sliding further toward dilapidation each year. Fortunately, in mid-2018 it was announced that the building would be renovated as Brennan's Work and Leisure, a multi-use space housing offices, cafés, and other lifestyle amenities.

A 1923 Franklin on exhibit at the New York International Auto Show. Courtesy Detroit Public Library.

View of men installing Goodrich tires road sign next to 1910 Franklin truck parked on roadside. The man wearing the suit and hat is supervising the workers; "Goodrich tires, pleasant traveled" logo on side of truck. Courtesy Detroit Public Library.

A young W. A. McNabb working at a drafting table on the design of a Franklin. Courtesy Detroit Public Library.

3016–18 LOCUST

Another of architect Preston Bradshaw's creations, the Gillham Motors Corporation Building was home to a series of automobile firms. The Gillham Motors Corporation moved into the building in 1921 to sell Studebakers, followed by the Ward-Battle Motor Company in 1922, a Chrysler dealership, the Orthwein Motor Corporation in 1925, followed by the Allen James Motor Company (1928), the Berry Motor Company (1929), and a used-car dealer through 1939.

The L. M. Stewart Inc. Used Car Department at 3016 Locust Street in 1935. © *St. Louis Post-Dispatch* and courtesy Missouri History Museum, St. Louis.

3021 LOCUST

The Velie Motor Vehicle Company started as a carriage builder and eventually manufactured cars, trucks, tractors, and airplanes. Headquartered in Moline, Illinois, the firm was started by Willard Velie, the grandson of John Deere of farm equipment fame. Velie automobiles were produced from 1908 to 1928, and remain prized by brass-era car buffs. When the firm closed, the aircraft arm was sold to St. Louisan Phil Ball, a backer of Charles Lindbergh.

3024 LOCUST

Chicago-based Vesta Accumulator Company, known after 1929 as the Vesta Battery Corporation, originally began life in 1897 manufacturing electrical parts for bicycles but quickly added automobiles to its target market. In 1913, it began opening branches across the country, and its St. Louis store was one of its first built.

3026—3028 LOCUST

Based in Little Rock, Arkansas, the Myar Manufacturing Company, automotive upholsterers specializing in creating seat covers, saw the boom in automotive manufacturing in St. Louis and had this building built in 1919. The clock on its façade could indicate Myar knew it was time to capitalize on the volume of vehicles being built in St. Louis.

3030 LOCUST

Dating to 1913, the Stearns-Knight Building was home to the Stearns-Knight Auto Company for four years. The Superior Motor Car Company moved into the building in 1918, followed by a succession of automobile and implement dealers until 1938, when a nonautomotive manufacturer moved in.

Henry Ford was actually caught caught on camera posing in an early Locomobile with his friend Ralzemond A. Parker near Woodward Avenue and 13 Mile Road in Royal Oak, Michigan, in 1923. Courtesy Detroit Public Library.

3029—3033 LOCUST

Built in 1911, this building was home to the Locomobile Company of Missouri until its departure in 1917. Designed by architect James E. Powers, the building has been home to a series of automotive and nonautomotive businesses over the last century.

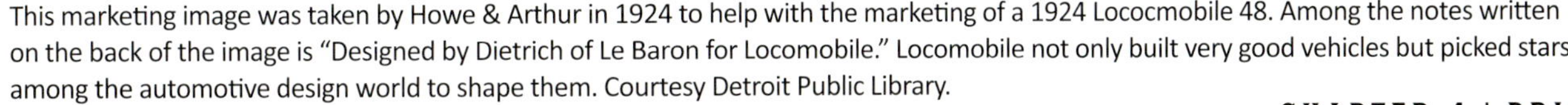

This marketing image was taken by Howe & Arthur in 1924 to help with the marketing of a 1924 Lococmobile 48. Among the notes written on the back of the image is "Designed by Dietrich of Le Baron for Locomobile." Locomobile not only built very good vehicles but picked stars among the automotive design world to shape them. Courtesy Detroit Public Library.

3039 LOCUST

Leach, Brouster, and Company chose Preston Bradshaw in late 1915 as the architect for its new sales showroom featuring Rauch and Lang electric, Baker electric, and Owen Magnetic cars. Despite Bradshaw's design and ornamentation of the attractive building, Leach-Brouster didn't last long and sold the building in 1918 to the Supreme Motor Company, St. Louis's Stutz Motor Company dealer. Even non-enthusiasts have heard of the famous Stutz Bearcat, a vehicle well-known for ruggedness and power. It is associated in the social consciousness with flappers, raccoon coats, and the excesses and vibrancy of the Roaring Twenties. Stutzes were sold from this location from 1918 to 1924. While the original Stutz Motor Company filed for bankruptcy in 1937, the magic associated with the name caused premier automobile designer Virgil Exner to bring a reincarnated Stutz Motor Car Company to life to sell custom sports cars (with General Motors running gear) in 1970. Highly idiosyncratic, these "new" Stutzes were popular with celebrities and other notables. At one point in the 1950s, this building housed the advertising department for Coca-Cola Bottling, and it is now an ice cream parlor.

3100 LOCUST

This white brick building featuring detailed terracotta ornamentation is all show on its front corner at Locust and North Compton but does its work on its east side with six garage openings. Built in 1916 for the DeLuxe Automobile Company to sell Oldsmobile cars and trucks—and yes, Olds did make trucks back then—the building is currently undergoing renovation.

3101–3111 LOCUST

Announcement of the establishment of the Tate-Gillham Motor Car Company (the predecessor of the Gillham Motors Corporation) as a Dodge distributor appeared in the November 26, 1914 issue of *The Automobile*. President Frank Ruben Tate was something of an innovator—among other things, he sought to increase sales by distributing newsletters full of motoring tips to customers, and to decrease costs by improving the process by which new cars were prepared for delivery. The firm was so successful that it had two locations on Locust, with the second building nearby at 3041–3043 Locust. Perhaps this success is reflected in the fact that Mr. Tate had already retired when he died of heart disease at the relatively young age of fifty-seven in 1934.

A 1932 Oldsmobile Six Convertible Roadster. Courtesy Detroit Public Library.

The Tate Motor Company building at 3101–3111 Locust remained associated with the automotive industry from its completion in 1918 until 1948. Courtesy Missouri History Museum, St. Louis.

3108 LOCUST

Architect H. W. Guth designed this showroom, completed in 1927 for the Olive Motor Company, in the Mission Revival style. It now hosts a bar and club.

3115 LOCUST

Arguably the best-known of St. Louis's "Little Three" manufacturers, the Moon Motor Car Company was an early resident of the Locust Automobile Row. In 1905, the Moon Brothers Carriage Company began producing automobiles at its factory located at the intersection of Main and Douglass streets. Success followed, and by 1925, the firm had six plants operating in St. Louis. A 1917 Moon advertisement places the "City Sales Department" at 3040 Locust, but the firm's showroom was at 3115 Locust by the beginning of the Roaring Twenties. Unfortunately, Moon fell victim to changing tastes and the Great Depression. The firm produced its last vehicle in 1930 and went into receivership the same year. As an unfortunate aside, the Moon Motor Company bankruptcy process remains the longest on record: the liquidation process wasn't completed until 1966. Nonetheless, Moon automobiles are highly prized in the collector car community.

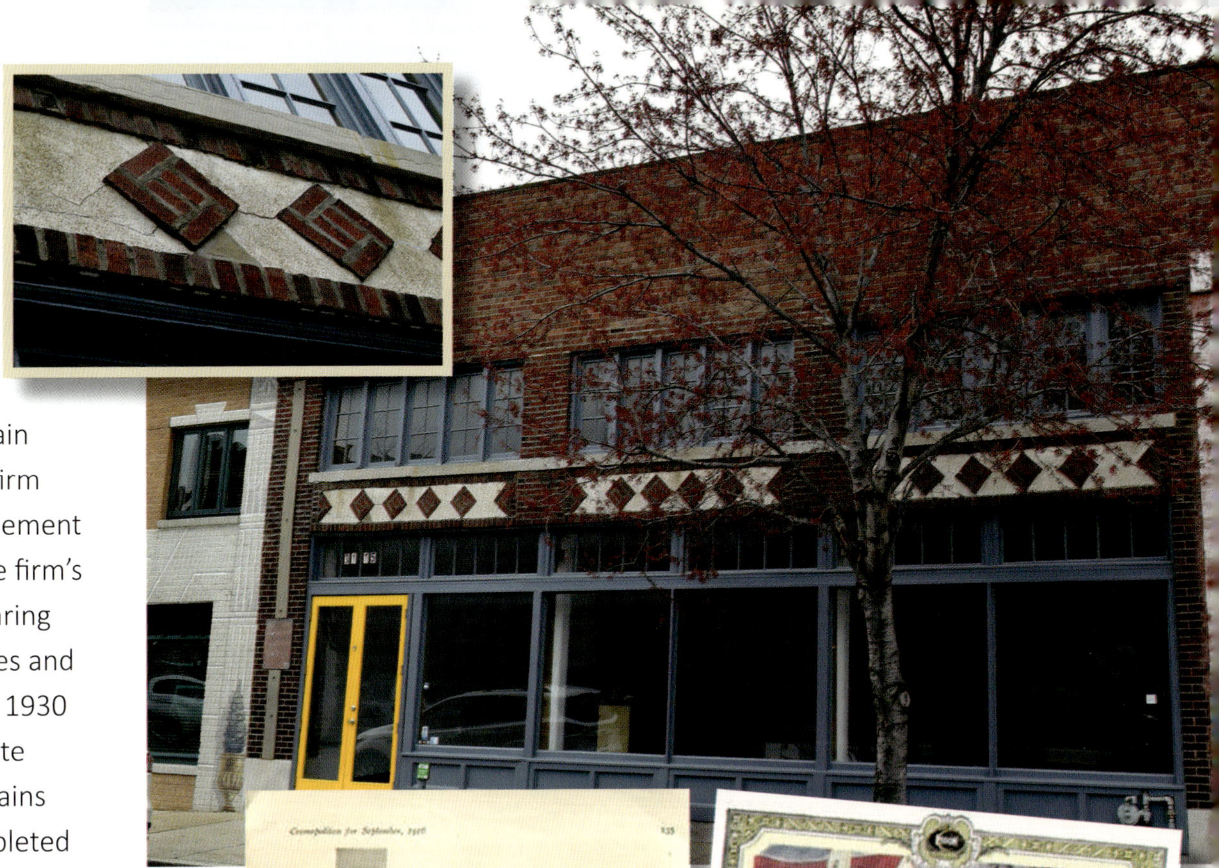

Moon Motor Car Company Stock Certificate

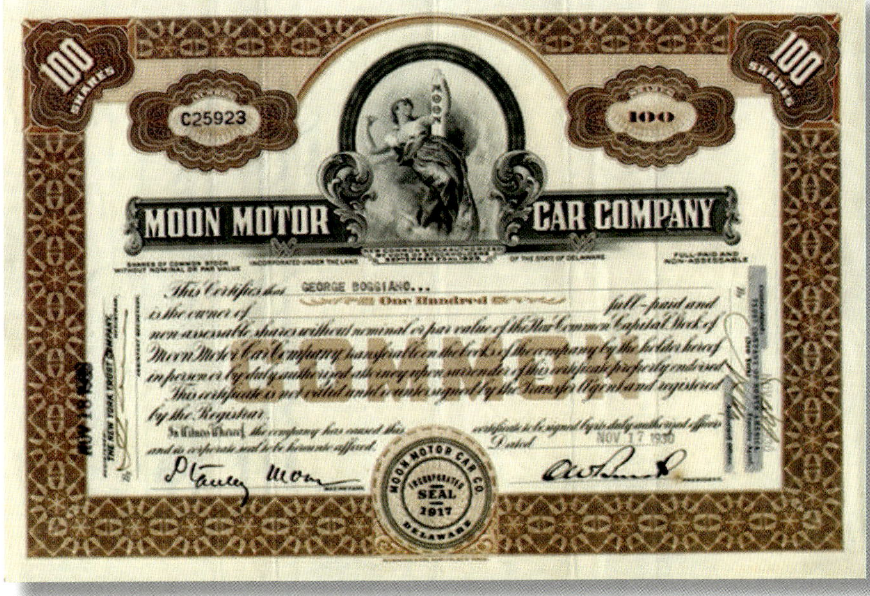

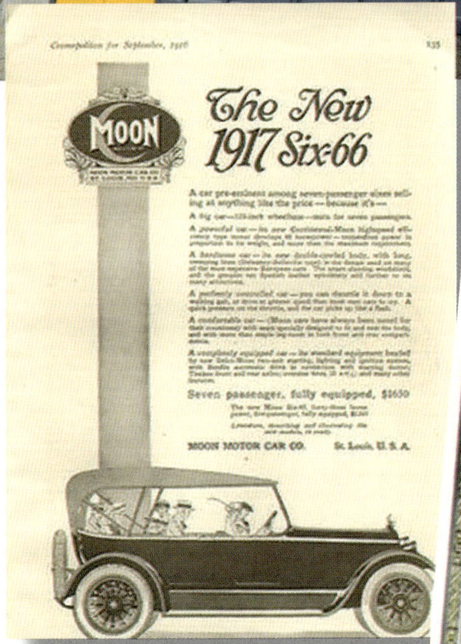

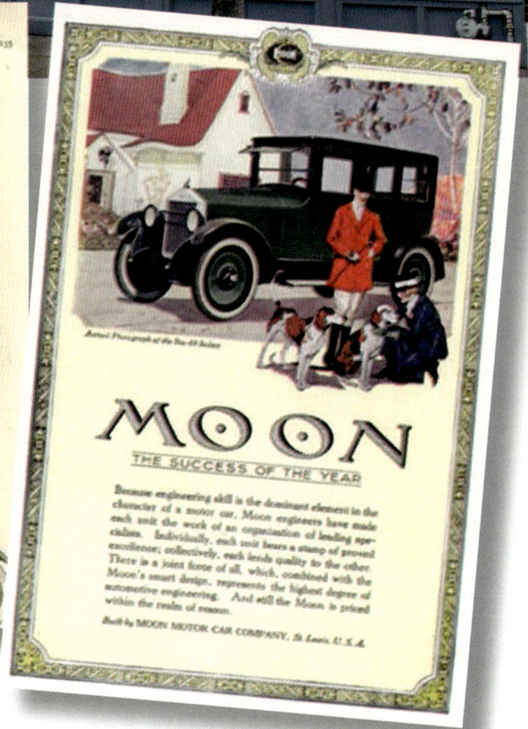

Moon Motor Car Company advertisements.

3116–3120 LOCUST

Champion Auto Springs called on the popular Preston Bradshaw to design its Locust Street building, completed in 1916. It features three storefronts, one of which includes a garage door for servicing and replacing springs.

3117–3119 LOCUST

The Reliable Auto Tire Company had a relatively long tenure on Automobile Row: it was housed at this address from 1918 to 1928. The Reifler Tire Company, in turn, occupied the building from 1933 through 1936. As with other Automobile Row sites, a series of assorted occupants followed.

An employee removes a 30 x 3 Firestone tire by hand in preparation for installing new rubber on the wheel. Courtesy Detroit Public Library.

3133—3135 LOCUST

Architect James E. Powers drew the plans for this building, constructed in 1911 for the Cochrane Motor Sales Company. It immediately began advertising the Cartercar, the "gearless car." Its friction-drive transmission—a precursor to today's continuously variable transmissions (CVTs)—were indeed innovative but only helped keep the Michigan-based manufacturer in business until 1915.

The new Cartercars of 1912 on display at a car show. Courtesy Detroit Public Library.

3137 LOCUST

Right after the Mississippi Valley Motor Company organized in 1916, it called upon Preston Bradshaw to design a new building for it at 3137 Locust. For the first Oakland and Pontiac dealer in St. Louis, sales from this location were successful enough to merit a move in 1924 to a larger building just up the street at 2801 Locust.

A circa 1911 photograph of the Oakland Motor Car Company factory in Pontiac, Michigan, taken next by Spooner & Wells, Inc., of Detroit. Note the railroad box cars serving parts to the plant. Courtesy Detroit Public Library.

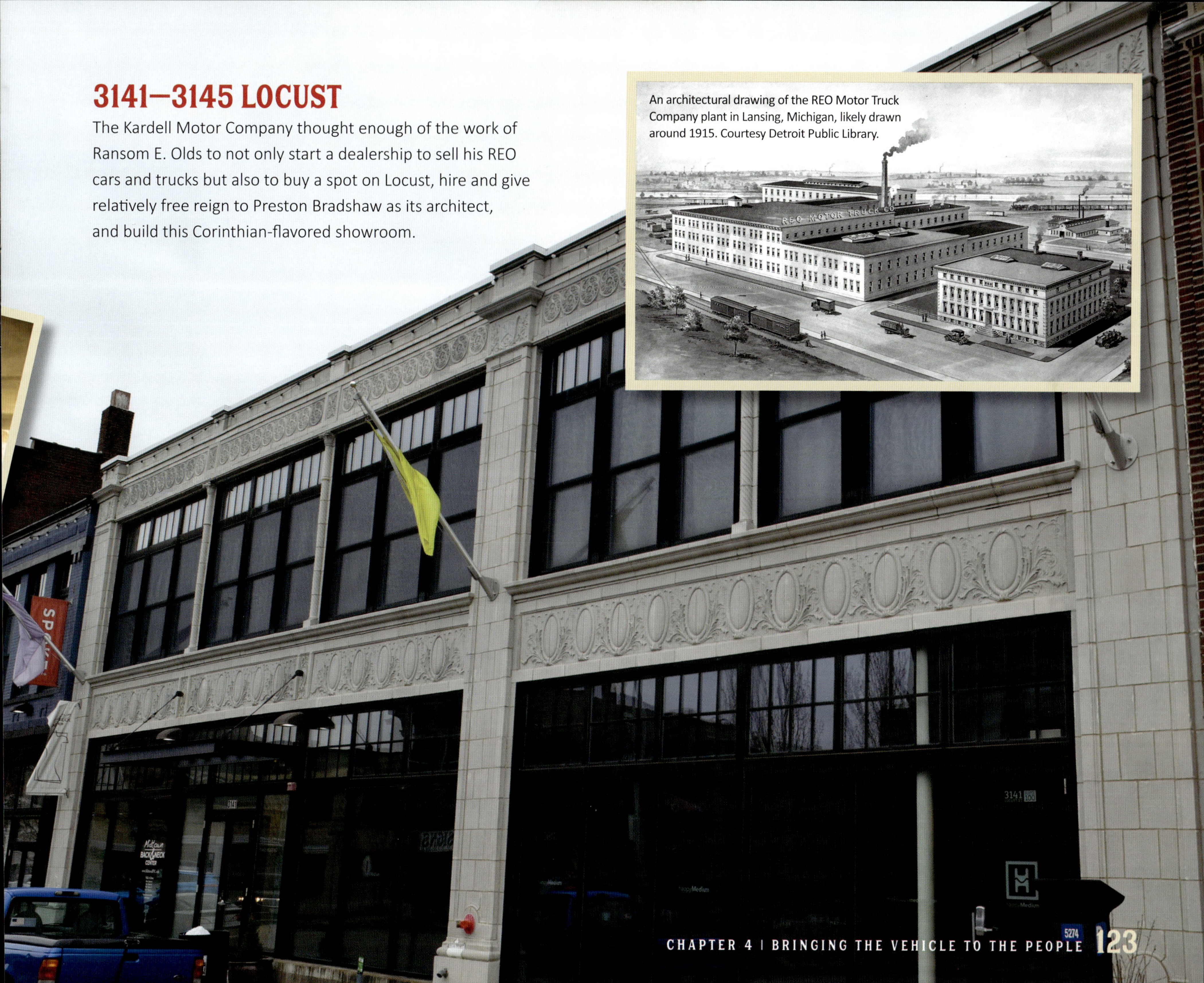

3141–3145 LOCUST

The Kardell Motor Company thought enough of the work of Ransom E. Olds to not only start a dealership to sell his REO cars and trucks but also to buy a spot on Locust, hire and give relatively free reign to Preston Bradshaw as its architect, and build this Corinthian-flavored showroom.

An architectural drawing of the REO Motor Truck Company plant in Lansing, Michigan, likely drawn around 1915. Courtesy Detroit Public Library.

3147—3149 LOCUST

Having new commercial buildings designed and built as a matching pair appealed to multiple automotive businesses on Locust, including the United States Tire Company. It hired Stephens and Pearson to design the buildings, which were completed by H. F. Nagel in 1912. By 1930, Climax-Jones & Quinn, Inc., had moved into the taller 3149 building and sold automotive and tractor parts. The details on the facades once matched, but both time and designs have altered them slightly.

Courtesy Missouri History Museum, St. Louis.

The art of adding tread to a tire.
Courtesy Detroit Public Library.

3150 LOCUST

The Independent Tire Company dovetailed on the success of the Koochook Rubber Company, which had started selling tires from 3152 Locust in 1912, by building the corner shop with a corner entrance next door eleven years later.

3200 LOCUST

A latecomer to Locust Street's Auto Row was Standard Auto Parts, and the timing of its arrival is evidenced by the modern design of its building. Architect Saul L. Reuben included a rounded second-story corner window in the buff brick building.

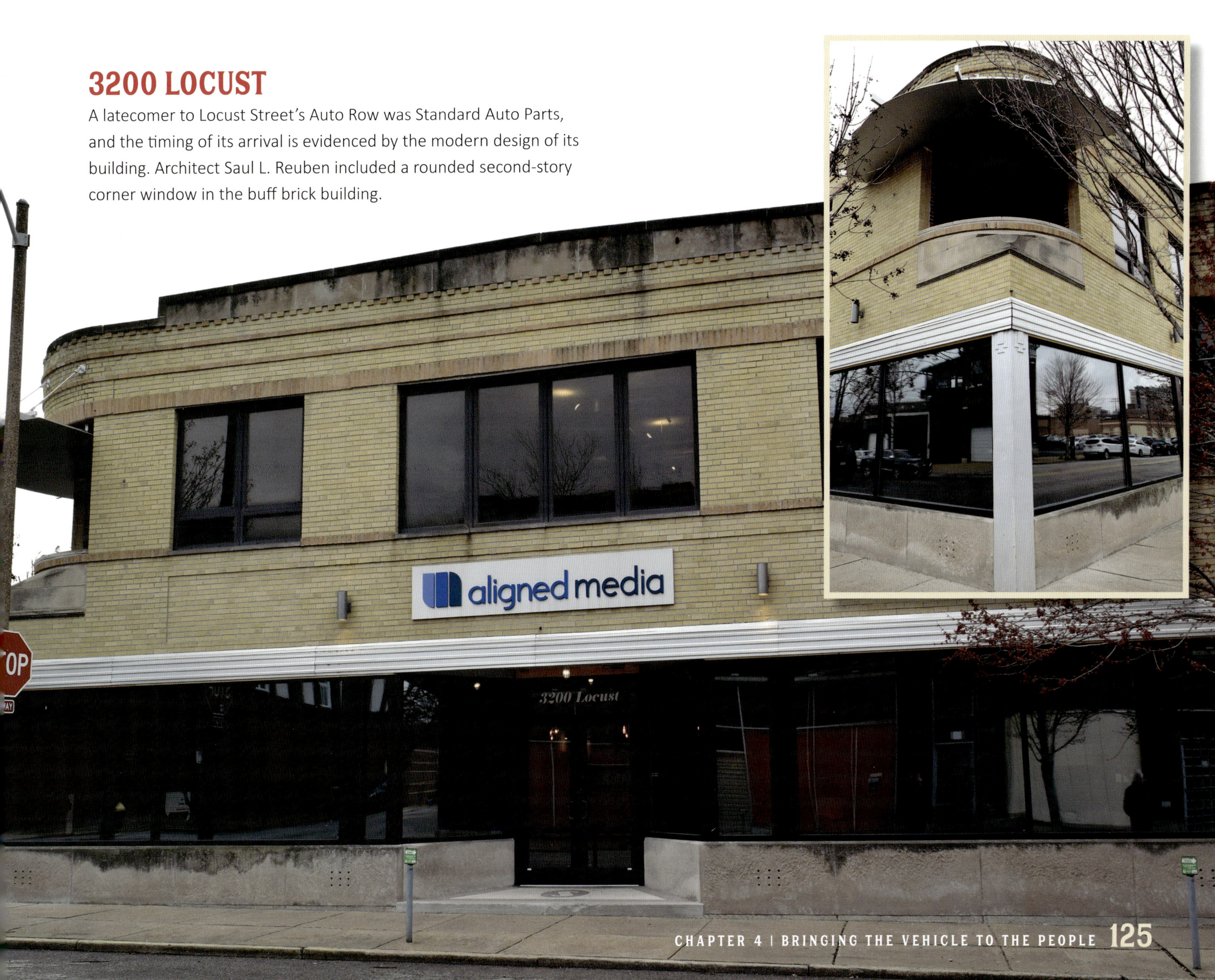

3201 LOCUST

Highly decorative when it was built in 1911, the first occupant of this building was the Firestone Tire and Rubber Company. A series of dealerships subsequently occupied the building, but undoubtedly one of the most idiosyncratic was the Durant Motors dealership, from 1924 to 1930. After making his (first) fortune as a carriage manufacturer, William C. Durant took control of the Buick Motor Company in 1904, and was then instrumental in forming General Motors in 1908. Unfortunately, financial troubles forced him out in 1910. After backing Louis Chevrolet, Durant regained control of GM in 1916. He was forced out again in 1920 and founded Durant Motors in 1921. The firm also fielded the Star brand from 1922 through 1928. But, as with so many other manufacturers, Durant Motors failed during the Great Depression, and Billy Durant died a poor man.

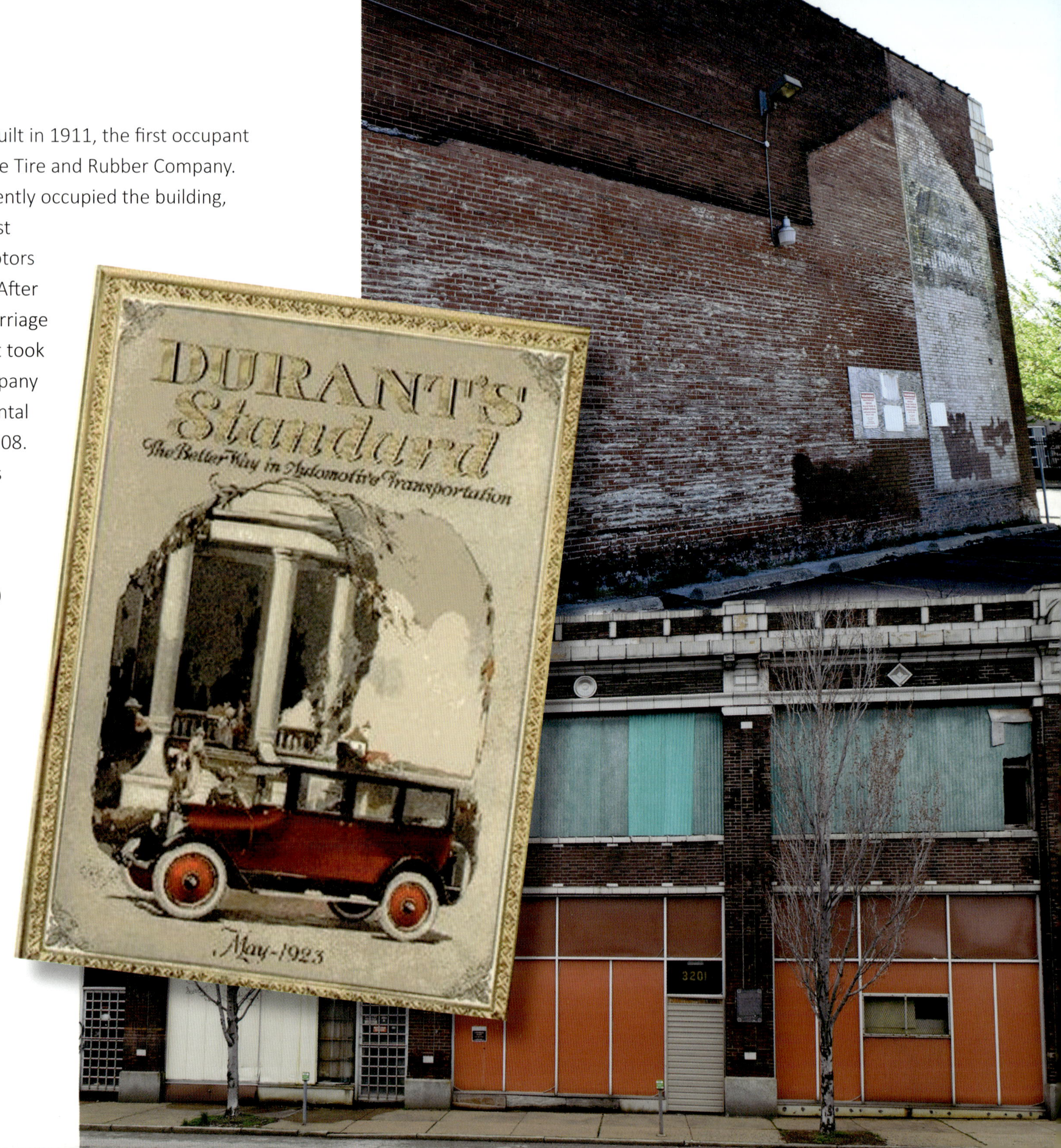

3216 LOCUST

Wagner Tire and Gear sold and advertised the availability of a variety of automotive parts from its store, including innovative Bock tapered roller bearings.

3212 LOCUST

From his showroom on Locust, Wooster Lambert changed the name of the company of which he was president, the Simplex Automobile Company, to the Motors Company in 1913 when he added sales of the Garford to the Simplex and King lines the dealership already sold.

An American Simplex, decorated with floral garlands and decked in silver, was in high style for its display in a trade show. A sign reading, "The Elsie Janis silver mounted American Simplex" was placed in front of the vehicle for this circa 1910 photograph taken by Spooner & Wells, Inc. Courtesy Detroit Public Library.

3219 LOCUST

The Universal Auto Parts store and shop not only retailed but worked on motor and gear parts for both road and agricultural vehicles. It prized its ability to "Kotherize" used pistons, meaning a machine would fire compressed lead shot inside each piston, expanding its skirt. The building no longer remains, but evidence of it survives in both photographs and building ghosts.

The front of the Universal Auto Parts store in 1935. Courtesy Missouri History Museum, St. Louis.

Employees of Universal Auto Parts working on pistons in 1935. Courtesy Missouri History Museum, St. Louis.

This group posed with a Plymouth outside the L. M. Stewart Chrysler dealership at 3228 Locust Street for an Isaac Sievers shot for © owner *St. Louis Post-Dispatch* in September 1934. Courtesy Missouri History Museum, St. Louis.

Two men posing with a Plymouth at L. M. Stewart, Inc., at 3228 Locust, in November 1932. © *St. Louis Post-Dispatch* and courtesy Missouri History Museum, St. Louis.

3222 LOCUST

The Cadillac-Chrysler Building stands as an architectural gem in midtown
St. Louis. According to the plaque placed on this building by the Horseless
Carriage Club of Missouri, growth of the Cadillac dealership
at its initial location down the street necessitated
the move to this larger site. Cadillacs were
sold here until 1930. Subsequently,
L. M. Stewart Chrysler dealership
into the building, and
after the war.

.ZACK
HOME OF
KRANZBERG ARTS
FOUNDATION
StoryTrack
Sophie's Lounge
Kelly & Associates, LLC
Socially Jen & Co.
Turn Restaurant

turn

SPEED
LIMIT
30

South Kingshighway

St. Louis's third "Automobile Row" developed on South Kingshighway in the city of St. Louis. Unlike the Locust Street and Delmar Boulevard rows, much of South Kingshighway, long considered an undeveloped outer road, was designed, built, and therefore paved in the automotive era and after streetcars had stopped servicing the street in 1915. Auto dealerships began popping up on South Kingshighway immediately after World War I. Among the early ones was the Brahm-Mitchellette Motor Car Company, which had a Spanish Revival–style dealership constructed at

3537 South Kingshighway in 1927. The size, stature, and success of Brahm-Mitchellette, which sold Oaklands and Pontiacs, set the trend of Kingshighway being dealership-oriented as opposed to automotive garages and retail stores. This beautiful building was used as a dealership for its first ten years, long housed an insurance company, and now includes offices and loft apartments.

Seeing the construction of that dealership, as well as recognizing the convenience and appeal of the wide, paved Kingshighway, the space it offered for parking lots, and the requirement of many

The Brahm-Mitchellette Motor Company at 3537 South Kingshighway Boulevard happily doesn't look much different today than it did when this photo was taken in August of 1931. © Brahm-Mitchellette Motor Company and courtesy Missouri History Museum, St. Louis.

A December 1939 view of the Joe Winkley Motor Sales building at 4300 South Kingshighway Boulevard. © Chrysler Corporation, Dodge Division, and courtesy Missouri History Museum, St. Louis.

manufacturers to use a standard dealership and service building design, led to a massive growth of dealerships along the road. By 1945, thirty-two dealerships lined South Kingshighway, while only three remained on Locust.

Notable dealerships along the road included McMahon Ford, Placke Chevrolet, Bender Best Lincoln-Mercury, King Dodge, Vincel Pontiac, Christopher-Southwest Motor Sales, and three Dave Sinclair Ford dealerships—one each for cars, trucks, and used vehicles. But by the late twentieth century, much of South Kingshighway followed the history of the city's earlier Automobile Rows, along with the migration of residents to St. Louis County and St. Charles County.

Today, automobile dealerships and garages dot the landscape across the St. Louis region. It would be difficult to identify one particular location as a modern "Automobile Row." Perhaps the most obvious difference in automobile retailing then and now is the development of the Carvana approach to car buying. According to its corporate webpage, "Carvana provides car shoppers a better way to buy a car. Browse used cars online and get approved for financing." Carvana's "auto vending machine" style of construction provides a stark contrast to the storefronts and showrooms that characterized Automobile Rows in St. Louis and throughout the country.

The service area inside the Crosby Motor Company dealership at 2323 South Kingshighway was photographed in the summer of 1937. © Chrysler Corporation and courtesy Missouri History Museum, St. Louis., Sievers, Isaac, 1886–1954

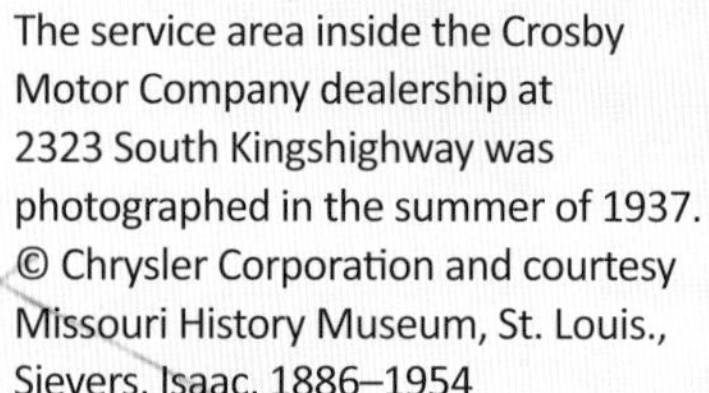

The service area of Crosby Motor Company at 2323 South Kingshighway in 1936. © Chrysler Corporation and courtesy Missouri History Museum, St. Louis.

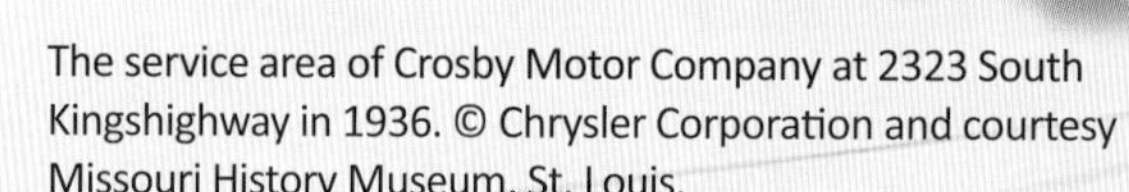

The Joe Winkley Motor Sales used car lot at 4300 South Kingshighway just before Christmas of 1939. © Chrysler Corporation, Dodge Division, and courtesy Missouri History Museum, St. Louis., Sievers, Isaac, 1886–1954

Schicker Ford at 3300 South Kingshighway.

The modern Don Brown Chevrolet dealership at 2244 South Kingshighway.

Charles Schmitt & Company at 3500 South Kingshighway, prior to becoming the Rolls-Royce dealer in 1971. c. 1970. Courtesy of John Sherman.

This 1955 photo of Hull-Dobbs Ford Sales and Service at 4315 South Kingshighway Boulevard shows the design of American automobiles in the twilight of the rounded fin years. © holder unknown and courtesy Missouri History Museum, St. Louis., Dorrill Studio.

DEALERSHIPS

Very few degrees of separation fall between most St. Louisans and any of a number of the city's automobile dealerships that have served St. Louis for more than a half-century. From print advertisements to stickers and license plate frames on vehicles to radio, television, and internet commercials immediately recognizable for music and catch-phrases, dealership names are almost as familiar as those of high schools and the Cardinals' starting rotation.

One of the very first dealerships in St. Louis and one of the first residents of Locust Street's automobile row, Weber Implement Company, was founded in 1902 by George Weber, and his descendants now operate three dealerships as Weber Chevrolet.

Peter Heutel literally went out to the country and opened a business on a gravel road when he founded the Sunset Auto Repair Company on Gravois Road in 1912. Four years later, he opened Sunset Ford, and his descendants still sell Fords on Gravois.

In 1912, when transportation was more commonly offered by horses than the newfangled horseless carriages, George Jacob Seeger opened a blacksmith shop on Olive Boulevard. The family added the sales and service of farm implements a few years later, and by the 1930s, sales of Nashes, Hudsons, and Chevrolets began. Seeger Toyota opened at the same location in 1969 and remains the oldest Toyota dealer in the state of Missouri.

John C. Auffenberg worked with the family business, Monarch Motors on Locust Street, before opening a Ford dealership at Enright and Kingshighway in 1940. He quickly added a second Ford dealership, this one in Belleville, Illinois, and started a family business that has now multiplied to nine dealerships in the St. Louis metropolitan area.

In 1940, John Londoff Sr. opened Londoff Motors on the second floor of his family's bowling alley and bar. While he initially chose to sell

Plymouths, the radical looks of the Ford Edsel convinced him to jump to Ford in 1958, and he took pride in being able to sell and becoming the city's top dealer of the historically unappealing Edsel. In 1960, he founded Johnny Londoff Chevrolet and quickly asked George Drake to write and Marty Ronson to sing an advertising jingle for the dealership. Now well over a half-century old, that jingle has been featured by the *Wall Street Journal* and *TIME Magazine* for its unmistakable catchiness.

The Suntrup family began selling cars in the St. Louis area in 1957, and the Suntrup Automotive Group now handles nine different makes at its dealerships throughout the St. Louis area.

The Mungenast Automotive Family opened its first car dealership in 1965 and has since expanded to not only four auto dealerships but also sales of motorcycles, all-terrain vehicles, and power equipment.

Former St. Louis City police officer Dave Sinclair joined South Kingshighway's automobile row when he opened a Ford dealership there in 1966. Sinclair later added Buick, GMC trucks, and Pontiac, becoming the largest Buick dealer in the state and one of the largest in the country as well as a leading Pontiac dealer.

Frank Bommarito began his career in the automotive sales industry as a car jockey at a local General Motors dealership before serving in the United States Navy for two years during the Korean War. After returning from the war, he climbed the ranks as a successful automotive salesman before opening an Oldsmobile dealership in 1971. The Bommarito Automotive Group, now with twenty locations selling twelve different makes of new and commercial trucks, is Missouri's largest automotive dealer group.

GMC DUKW vehicles, many likely built in St. Louis, and an M4 Sherman tank arriving ashore during World War II. Courtesy Missouri History Museum, St. Louis.

FIGHTING THE WAR
FROM THE FACTORIES

From almost the moment Japan started bombing Pearl Harbor in Hawaii on December 7, 1941, employees of automotive industries and factories in St. Louis and across the United States, knew many things would change, including at work. From the registration of more than ten million American men for the military draft during the war to the need for military as opposed to civilian transportation, World War II altered both what was built in auto-related plants and who worked in them between late 1941 and early 1946.

The Chevrolet light truck plant in St. Louis was given the task of building the CCKW 6-wheel-drive, 2.5-ton trucks intended to operate as tactical vehicles in all terrain and weather conditions. The ladder-framed trucks featured a GM 270-cubic-inch overhead valve and inline six-cylinder engine with ninety-one horsepower. Second only to the Jeep in popularity, 562,750 CCKWs were built for the war, and of those, 149,135 were built in St. Louis. While most were badged GMC, all but the final thousand built in St. Louis had Chevy axles.

Cargo dump trucks were also on the "to build" list for Chevrolet's St. Louis plant, and 37,803 were built there on the CCKW chassis.

The St. Louis Chevrolet plant was also assigned to build the GMC-designed 6.6 Amphibious Trucks, known as the DUKW. St. Louis

A CCKW 353 long chassis truck that served in the "Red Ball Express" transporting supplies over the two hundred miles between Cherbourg and Chartres, France, for three months following D-Day in June 1944. In those months, nearly six thousand trucks carried nearly a million tons of supplies and wore out over fifty thousand tires.

A Marine Corps motor detachment with their CCKW trucks in New River, North Carolina, in May 1942. Courtesy Library of Congress.

A GMC CCKW cargo dump truck. Courtesy Library of Congress.

built 6,748, or 32 percent, of the total 21,147 built. GMC built the sheet metal "boat" section in its Pontiac, Michigan, plant, and it subcontracted the assembly work to Chevrolet. However, the "ducks" carried GMC identification tags. Three-quarters of a century after they were built, many ducks remain in service as tourism boats all over the world, though they are military vehicles built decades before modern passenger boating safety standards now operating well past their intended service life.

A "duck" landing in southern France in 1944. Courtesy World War II Database.

The St. Louis Car Company built gliders, the flying boat seaplane, and tracked landing vehicle (LVTs or "Alligators"), continuing its long trend of expanding beyond streetcar and interurban production.

An LVT-1 carries Marines to the front in Bougainville in 1943. Courtesy Associated Press.

Troops deploying from an LVT "Alligator" on Saipan Beach. Courtesy World War II Database.

A Marine Corps motor detachment with their CCKWs in New River, North Carolina.

GMC CCKW Cargo Dump.

The Chevrolet Corvette prototype
debuted at the 1953 Autorama.

Chapter Six

POSTWAR BOOM

. . . AND BUST

"St. Louis, with its three big automotive plants turning out some 700,000 cars and trucks a year, may be only No. 2 in the country now. Someday, maybe, it will be No. 1."
—Robert E. Hannon, *St. Louis Commerce Magazine*, November 1966 issue.

"It is difficult to make predictions—especially about the future."

—Old Danish proverb

During the years following World War II, St. Louis stayed as close to the center of the country's trend as to the center of the country geographically. As soldiers returned home after victory, and as technology, industry, retail, and design shifted from wartime needs to a consumer market fueled by new peace and prosperity, the automotive industry changed lanes in the Gateway to the West.

Automotive builders native to the city had disappeared a decade before the war began, but Chevrolet remained in St. Louis and expanded production. Ford wanted to return to the area, and Chrysler wanted to enter it. While the Chevrolet assembly plant at Union and Natural Bridge continued building trucks and A-body cars, it soon became the home of Corvette production. Ford and Chrysler followed people out of the city of St. Louis to the county.

Chevrolet Chooses St. Louis to Build the Corvette

General Motors (GM) designer Harley Earl, who had helped design the 1927 LaSalle, the 1939 Buick Y-Job concept car, and the 1948 Cadillac, the first vehicle to feature tail fins, was keenly aware of the sports cars being built and road raced in England and the rest of Europe and felt the United States needed its own comparable and competitive vehicle. He offered "Project Opel" to Ed Cole, who hopped on the opportunity to design and develop an American sports car from the road up.

Cole's team quickly realized the use of glass-reinforced plastic (GRP, or fiberglass) bodies in Project Opel would render not only lighter body weights but also an immense cost savings for GM, as the tool and die costs for a conventional metal body would be $4.5 million versus $400,000 for GRP. The team quickly sculpted a modern two-seat roadster body fitted to a steel frame and a drive train utilizing a 3.9-liter or 235-cubic-inch displacement (cid) inline six-cylinder motor and two-speed automatic transmission. The car, christened "Chevrolet Corvette," made its inaugural appearance in New York City on January

The Corvette concept introduced at the General Motors Motorama, New York City, January 1953. Courtesy General Motors.

17, 1953, during the General Motors Autorama. While the general reaction to the car, and particularly its styling, was quite positive, many were disappointed the car featured merely a small six-cylinder motor.

A Russian immigrant with experience gained from auto and motorcycle racing in Berlin felt compelled to write a letter to then-GM president Ed Cole, expressing a number of suggested improvements to the Corvette. Cole immediately offered a job to the letter writer, Zora Arkus-Duntov, with the Corvette team at Chevrolet. Fortunately for GM as well as sports car owners and fans, Arkus-Duntov accepted.

Zora Arkus-Duntov in a 1957 Corvette, one of the first to feature fuel injection. Courtesy Detroit Public Library.

Beginning in the summer of 1953, Chevrolet produced a limited run of 300 Corvettes hand-built in Flint, Michigan, and named the C1 generation. They featured Polo White exterior paint, red interiors, and black tops and stickered for $3,470 without destination charges. Records indicate the first two Corvettes were retained by GM for testing and then scrapped. GM determined the impending success of the Corvette required the establishment of a new factory for its construction, and an old building in a corner of the 175-acre Chevrolet plant in north St. Louis was chosen.

Built in 1920 at the corner of Union Boulevard and Natural Bridge Avenue, the brick building chosen to be the home of the Corvette assembly lines had been nicknamed "The Mill," as it was designed and built to be the site for milling wood side panels for Fisher Body to be used for Chevrolets of the 1920s. It featured wood-block flooring for soaking oil and grease, small rooms, and numerous narrow, dead-end hallways, and the renovations of the building for Corvette assembly never overcame its inherent design flaws. The building still had a hole in its roof through which snow fell when Corvettes were first built in it.

Four areas were distinguished for Corvette assembly within the building, one each for the body shop, paint, chassis, and trim. The vehicles' subassemblies met on a central line, and the GRP bodies were assembled in an area of merely 200 by 500 feet, beginning with the underbody and its 180 pre-drilled holes. The radiator, steering column, and wiring harness were then installed in each body, followed by the seats, upholstery, and folding tops, which were now tan rather than the Flint black. A hoist would then lift each body and mate it to a chassis.

Chevrolet's Blue Flame inline six-cylinder engines with 150 horsepower were shipped from Michigan to St. Louis, where the carburetor, ignition, and transmission were added. The engines were then tested on three dynamometer machines for thirty minutes before being added to the completed body and chassis. The rear wheels were spun and balanced by machines installed at the end of the assembly line that had been invented and integrated specifically for construction of the Corvette. Employees would then drive the Corvettes off the line and test them on the grounds of the plant before loading them onto automotive carriers to be transported by rail.

The first Corvette built in St. Louis was completed on a Friday afternoon in December 1953. The plant could at first build only one car per day but by the end of the same month had increased production to three per day. Fourteen 1954 Corvettes were built in St. Louis in

A view of rows of 1957 Chevrolet Corvette cars parked in the lot of the Chevrolet factory in St. Louis, Missouri. The label on the back of the image reads: "Largest shipment yet of Corvettes equipped with Chevrolet's exclusive Ramjet fuel injection left the St. Louis plant of the company this week. The number, posed in the yard outside the assembly building, was (count 'em) fifty. They were destined for all parts of the country where demand for the model far exceeds the supply. Fuel injection, being pioneered by Chevrolet in its 1957 line, replaces the conventional carburetor and assures quicker, smoother accelerator response. With the device, Chevrolet's new 283 cubic inch V8 develops 283 horsepower." Courtesy Detroit Public Library.

December 1953. By June 1954, the St. Louis plant could build fifty Corvettes each day, and the price of each car had dropped to $2,774.

The racing in Zora Arkus-Duntov's European background began to influence the Corvette not long after its assembly birthplace moved to St. Louis. Arkus-Duntov introduced a new 4.3-liter, 265-cid V-8 motor capable of 195 horsepower in 1955, and a six-cylinder motor was no longer offered. When Arkus-Duntov's team added fuel injection in 1957, the Corvette became the first production car in the world to offer one horsepower for every inch of its engine's displacement.

One of the greatest years in American automotive history design

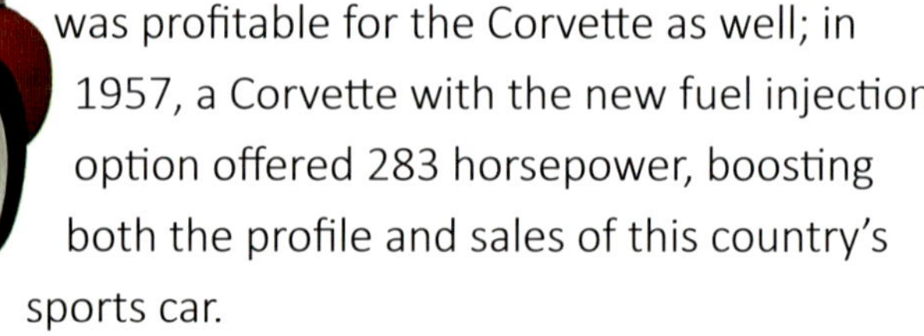

A 1957 Chevrolet Corvette. Courtesy General Motors.

was profitable for the Corvette as well; in 1957, a Corvette with the new fuel injection option offered 283 horsepower, boosting both the profile and sales of this country's sports car.

And while GM began a largely unpopular redesign of many of its cars in 1958, the Corvette entered its notable dual headlight phase and added quad tail-lights in 1961.

An entirely new design era began in 1963 with the introduction of the C2 Sting Ray with its large rear window—so large it could be split in two panes. While the split window lasted only one year, the model remains a favorite among Corvette aficionados.

A promotional shot for a 1960 Corvette with fuel injection. Courtesy General Motors.

The renowned 1963 Chevrolet Corvette Sting Ray with the split window. Courtesy National Corvette Museum.

Pilot Assembly Line

Photographers followed pieces and parts that came together in the
St. Louis assembly plant to become 1963 Chevrolet Corvette Sting Rays.
Courtesy Dean's Garage.

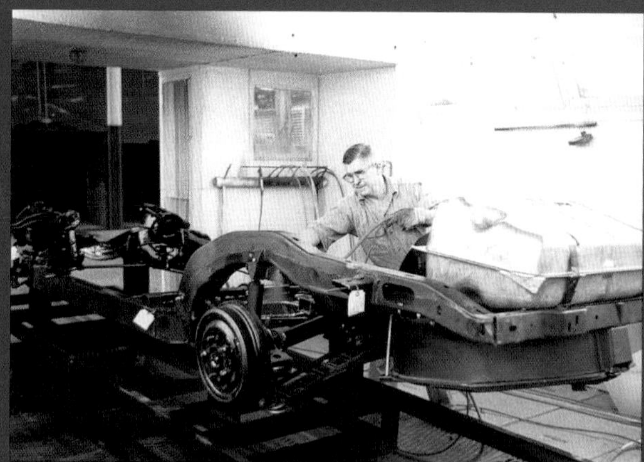

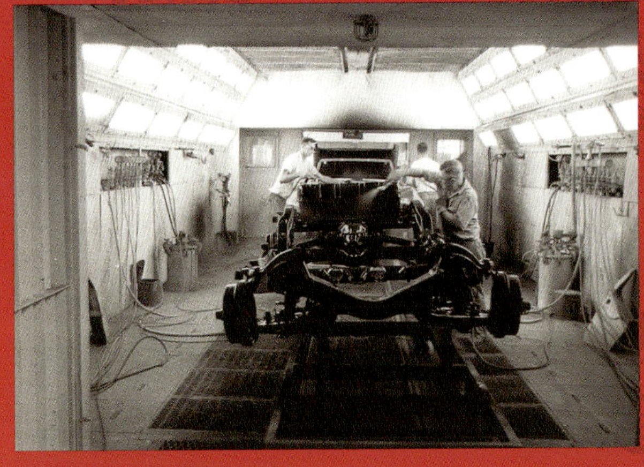

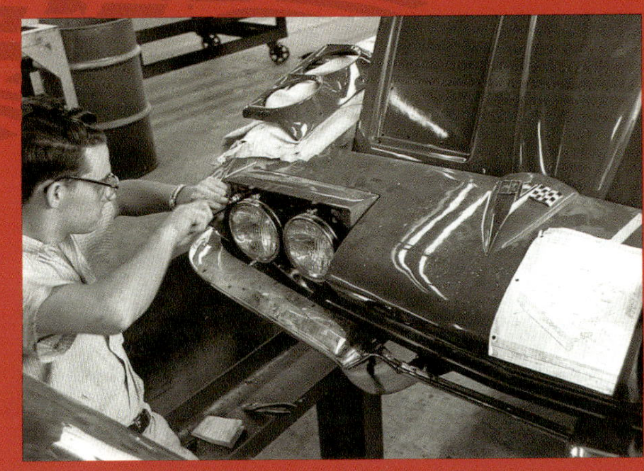
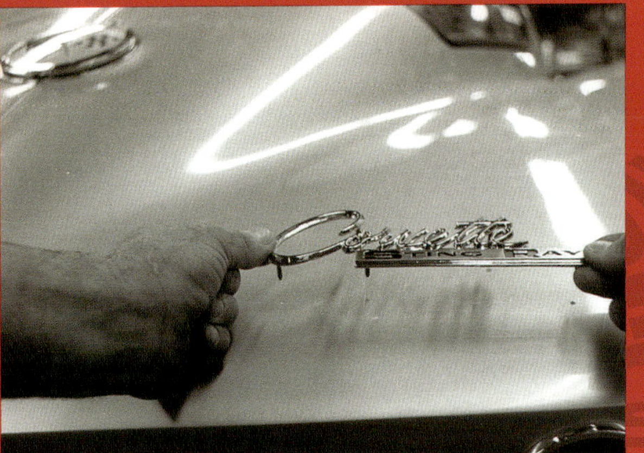

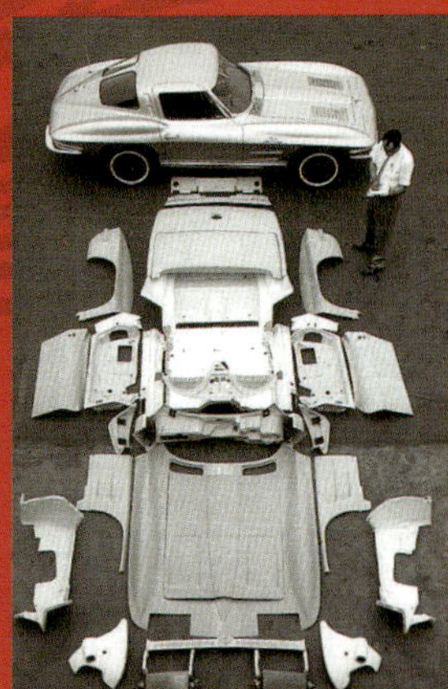

Members of the Omaha Tangier Shrine took a photo op immediately after taking delivery of their new 1965 Corvettes, which had an "RPO" (regular production option) for paint. The Omaha Tangier unit used the Corvettes—each personally purchased—in fundraising events to support children's health care.

In 1965, Arkus-Duntov began leading Corvette's engineering team through the creation of a new RPO package. In early 1967, the team's creation was race-ready, and it debuted on April 1, 1967, at the 12 Hours of Sebring. The Sunray team of Dave Morgan and Don Yenko won the GT class and finished twelfth overall. This led to the creation of the factory-only optional L88 option, included in merely twenty 1967 Corvettes, so GM could prove the car eligible for SCCA A-production and FIA GT events. In total, GM sold only about two hundred total L88 coupes and convertibles between 1967 and 1969, when the option was killed by more stringent emissions standards. While the L88 was advertised as having 435 horsepower, in reality it offered between 540 and 580 horsepower, and heavier options such as air conditioning and radios were not allowed to be included on L88 RPO cars.

Larry Shinoda's Mako Shark II concept car influenced the design of the C3 Corvettes beginning in 1968. While rear storage space was eliminated in the cars, removable roof panels were added, and a three-speed automatic transmission replaced the two-speeds.

Chevrolet made "Stingray" one word in its marketing of the 1969 Corvettes, whose standard V-8 motors were now 5.7-liter, 350-cid V-8s with 300 horsepower.

The 1970 Corvettes were the last to be untouched by changes to emissions standards by the Environmental Protection Agency, and the optional 5.7-liter of that year featured 370 horsepower, while the 7.4-liter, 454-cid LS5 motor offered 390 horsepower.

Reduced octane requirements of the 1971 Corvette caused the base motor's horsepower to begin to drop, while the optional LS6 big-block offered 425 horsepower. In 1973, the first year for a body-colored front urethane bumper, the base V-8 had 190 horsepower, and the optional big-block had 275 horsepower. The 1974 eliminated chrome bumpers on the Corvette altogether by adding a urethane rear bumper cover.

Model year 1975 could be interpreted as a low point for the Corvette, as the big-block motor option and convertibles were no longer offered, and the addition of federally required catalytic converters lowered the base 5.7-liter engine horsepower to 165. Revising that motor's intake in 1976 increased its horsepower to 180.

A promotional brochure issued by GM for the 1965 Corvette. Courtesy General Motors.

1968 Corvette. Courtesy General Motors.

1968 Corvette. Courtesy General Motors.

The body of a 1969 Corvette being placed on its chassis in the St. Louis plant. Courtesy Jim and Chester's Garage.

A fastback-styled rear end was integrated in the design for the 1978–1982 Corvettes, and the 1978 was chosen as the Indy 500 Pace Car. Three hundred replica Pace Cars were sold featuring a distinctive black and silver paint scheme with pace car graphics.

The changes in federal pollution and emissions standards that had drastically affected the Corvettes of the 1970s also affected the over half-century-old building in which they were built. Faced with making very expensive modifications to the old "Mill" building in St. Louis, GM began looking for more affordable alternatives and eyed a former Chrysler air conditioning plant in Bowling Green, Kentucky.

After considering the costs associated with upgrading the old buildings of the Chevrolet plant in north St. Louis as well as tax incentives offered by the city of Bowling Green, GM determined to close the St. Louis complex; build a new factory in Wentzville, Missouri, for constructing only vans; and move the expensive Corvette assembly line to Kentucky. The new building was twice the size of The Mill in St. Louis, and GM spent fourteen months upgrading it before the first Corvette left its assembly line on June 1, 1981. The St. Louis plant, which at one point had almost three million square feet of building floor space and was the largest assembly complex in the US automotive industry, was sold by GM in 1987.

The last Corvette to be built in St. Louis left the assembly line on July 31, 1981, and featured a beige exterior with a camel interior, an automatic transmission, aluminum wheels, and a removable roof. A plate marked "The Last St. Louis Corvette" was installed inside the right front fender, and many employees left signatures on the car's frame and chassis. Over a thousand photographs were taken to document the assembly of the car, and it was immediately purchased by and has remained in the hands of collectors. When it sold at auction in 2010, it had fourteen miles on the odometer.

Many former St. Louis Corvette builders waited for the completion of the new plant in Wentzville, thirty-four miles west of the St. Louis plant, but as construction delays began to mount—and with the end of unemployment benefits approaching—more employees took note of the United Auto Workers' reminder they had the right to claim jobs at other GM plants throughout the nation. Despite not knowing what they might find in Bowling Green, almost 950 former Chevrolet plant

A few of the over 800 ventilators and smokestacks at the General Motors Corporation plant in St. Louis in 1970. Courtesy *St. Louis Post-Dispatch*.

The 1977 Corvette. Courtesy General Motors.

The 1979 Corvette. Courtesy General Motors.

Despite the age of The Mill building and the difficult working conditions—hundred-degree days in the summer, freezing temperatures in the winter, daily scratches from raw fiberglass, and hazardous industrial air quality—St. Louisans built 695,214 Corvettes during a span of twenty-seven years. The Mill has since been demolished, and many of the St. Louis Corvette employees who moved to Bowling Green almost forty years ago now call it home, but over a quarter-century of the history of the greatest American sports car is directly tied to St. Louis.

employees in St. Louis chose to make the move 280 miles southeast.

When they arrived in Bowling Green, the former St. Louisans found that GM, incorrectly assuming the Wentzville plant would be finished on time and St. Louisans would stay and work in it, had unwittingly trained 750 residents of Warren County, Kentucky, and promised them jobs at the new Corvette plant. Resentment toward the transplanted St. Louis workers was made apparent in the Bowling Green area, as St. Louisans found prices on real estate and appliances were sometimes raised for them and law enforcement pulled them over and ticketed them for having Missouri rather than Kentucky license plates. Their higher wages and the fact that many initially left their families behind in St. Louis to sell homes and finish academic years deepened the mistrust by locals. African Americans who had moved from urban St. Louis to rural and largely Caucasian Warren County in Kentucky faced unique challenges, complicated by the fact their union wages established a new black middle class previously unseen in a right-to-work state.

The last Corvette built in St. Louis. Courtesy *St. Louis Post-Dispatch*.

St. Louis Chevrolet Plant in 1958.

End of an Era

GM CLOSES PLANT ON UNION AND NATURAL BRIDGE AFTER 67 YEARS

In 1955 the *St. Louis Post-Dispatch* proclaimed the city as "second only to Detroit" in the volume of automobiles produced, due in large part to the prodigious production of the "North Side" plant located at the intersection of Union Boulevard and Natural Bridge Avenue. The plant produced 13.3 million vehicles over its life and, at its peak in the late 1970s, employed over ten thousand people.

By the mid-80s, the facility was beginning to show its age. Modernization would be prohibitively costly, and years of growing labor-management discord had begun to disrupt productivity. As

St. Louis Chevrolet Plant in 1946.
Courtesy Missouri History Museum,
St. Louis.

The General Motors plant evolved from 1920 to the early 1960s, as did the vehicles it produced.

a result, GM management added the plant to its list of potential closures. One article in the *St. Louis Post-Dispatch* called the plant "a victim of its nearly sixty-seven years and expensive environmental defects" while another described it as "a filthy hotbox" and a site of suspicious fires and acts of sabotage.

Ultimately, the assembly plant closed in August 1987. Today, the old GM plant has been successfully converted into a business park.

The last sedan built by the St. Louis plant, a 1985 Ford Crown Victoria, leaves the assembly line.

In August 1946, one of the first pieces of metal framing is installed for the new Ford St. Louis Assembly Plant in Hazelwood, Missouri. Courtesy *St. Louis Post-Dispatch*.

After the plant's twenty-eight hundred workers built the last sedan to leave the plant in 1985—a Mercury Grand Marquis—over three hundred million dollars were spent on robotics and other upgrades to the plant before it began building the Ford Aerostar minivan. Reflecting another but more notable change in automotive tastes, the plant began building the Ford Explorer and Mercury Mountaineer, popular members of the exploding sport utility vehicle (SUV) club, in 1995.

The Hazelwood plant had joined two automotive waves toward the end of the twentieth century: the minivan introduced by Chrysler in the mid-1980s and the sport utility vehicle introduced by Ford itself

Ford hadn't really "left" St. Louis. Although it had closed its plant at 4100 Forest Park in 1942, it still owned the 345 acres it had bought in 1937 in Hazelwood, a suburb northwest of the city. According to the *St. Louis Post-Dispatch*, local residents had initially considered forming a village to be called "Motorville," but sanity prevailed and the newly formed municipality was christened Hazelwood. And by the time Benson Ford, a twenty-nine-year-old grandson of Henry Ford, stood in front of a twelve-million-dollar new factory at 6250 North Lindbergh on September 21, 1948, and told twenty-five hundred employees and five hundred dignitaries that new days and ways were being embraced by the company, 1949 Mercury coupes and sedans were already being built in the building behind him.

A photo of the Ford St. Louis plant taken in 2006. Courtesy *St. Louis Post-Dispatch*.

Ford, "Motorville" and Hazelwood

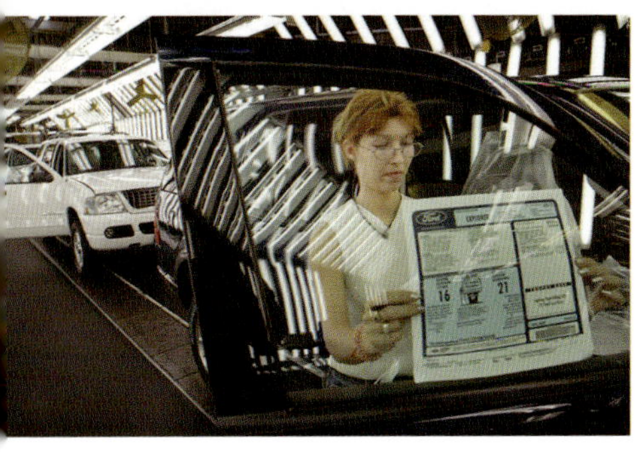

Christal Barnett-Politte finishes the metal on the hood of a Ford Explorer in October 2003. A new Ford Explorer's window sticker is applied before it leaves the assembly line in October 2003. Photos courtesy *St. Louis Post-Dispatch*.

in 1990 as a 1991 model Ford Explorer. In 1986, the Hazelwood plant began building the Ford Aerostar minivan, and in 1995 it started building the immensely popular Ford Explorer and Mercury Mountaineer sport utility vehicles. However, the incredible popularity of both vehicles, particularly the Explorer, inspired other automotive manufacturers to add sport-utes to their line-ups. As the variety and popularity of those vehicles, especially those built by GM, Honda, and Toyota, began to eat into the Explorer and Mountaineer numbers, and the Hazelwood plant showed its age in more and more ways, Ford made the decision to leave automotive manufacturing in St. Louis. The last Explorer rolled off the Hazelwood assembly line on March 8, 2006. In operation for nearly six decades, Ford closed this plant as part of its "Way Forward" corporate strategy. The plant buildings were subsequently demolished, and while the site is now being redeveloped as the Aviator Business Park, much of the original Ford plant site remains vacant.

The Big 3—Ford-Hazelwood current images.

Aviator Business Park at Hazelwood Ford Plant Site. Courtesy Gray Design Group.

Chrysler Joins the Party

In the 1970s, the Fenton plant stayed in the largely midsize category with the Volare/Aspen, Diplomat, Caravelle, and LeBaron. It switched back to economy with coupe versions of the famous K-cars, the Plymouth Reliant and Dodge Aries, that, along with a bailout by the federal government and the corporate leadership of Lee Iacocca, helped revive Chrysler after it nearly declared bankruptcy in 1979. Unfortunately, neither the K-cars nor Mr. Iacocca could save Chrysler from bankruptcy thirty years later.

The St. Louis South plant stayed with automobiles throughout the 1980s and switched in 1991 to building long wheelbase versions of the revolutionary and incredibly popular minivans, the Dodge Caravan and Plymouth Voyager, that Chrysler had introduced in November 1983.

The St. Louis North plant opened in 1966 and concentrated on building B-series Dodge Ram vans and wagons until 1980, when it shifted to building Ram trucks. It focused on the Ram 1500 half-ton truck and, later, Rams with Cummins diesel engines

Images of the Chrysler St. Louis South plant taken in June 1960. Courtesy Missouri History Museum, St. Louis.

1968 Charger on the St. Louis Assembly Line. Courtesy Chrysler Motors.

Chrysler manufactured almost every type of modern automobile in its conjoined plants on the north side of both Route 66 and Interstate 44 in Fenton, Missouri, southwest of downtown St. Louis. The first of the two plants built, the St. Louis South Plant, opened in 1959 and first built mainstream Plymouth and Dodge cars, but in 1960, it shifted its focus to the newly popular American compact car by building the Plymouth Valiant and the Dodge Lancer or Dart. Its cars shifted up in both size and speed when it added the Belvedere/Monaco/Coronet and the Plymouth Barracuda in 1964 and the Dodge Charger in 1968.

The Big 3—Chrysler plant current photos.

and the innovative V-10 gas engine. For a time, it was also the exclusive producer of RamBox-equipped trucks and eventually the Ram 1500 and 2500 single- and quad-cab pickup trucks.

By the early 2000s, total employment in the Fenton plants reached approximately sixty-two hundred people. Unfortunately, subsequent financial reverses (not the least of which was Chrysler's bankruptcy filing in 2009!) resulted in production shifting elsewhere, and the Fenton plant was shuttered. The site has been redeveloped as the Fenton Logistics Park and is currently signing new tenants.

Fenton Logistics Park on Chrysler Plant Site in Fenton.

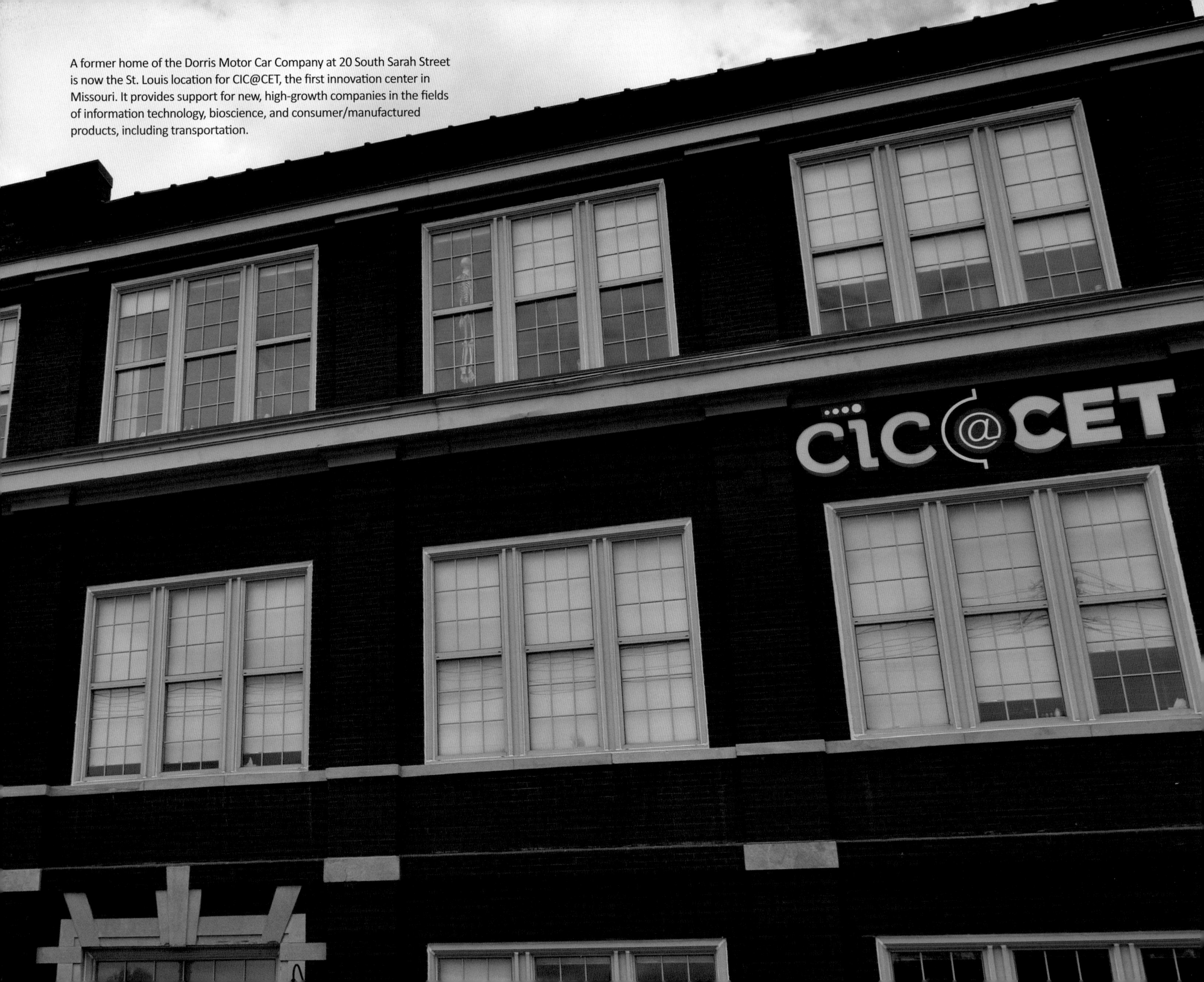
A former home of the Dorris Motor Car Company at 20 South Sarah Street is now the St. Louis location for CIC@CET, the first innovation center in Missouri. It provides support for new, high-growth companies in the fields of information technology, bioscience, and consumer/manufactured products, including transportation.

Chapter Seven

TOMORROW'S WHEELS
IN AN OLD CAR TOWN

St. Louis and the Automobile Industry—Then and Now

The automobile industry has come full circle. At its beginnings at the turn of the twentieth century, the American automobile industry consisted of dozens (and ultimately, hundreds!) of manufacturers and would-be manufacturers. Consumers could choose from vehicles powered by a number of different technologies: steam, electricity, or internal combustion. It has been estimated that more than one hundred steam vehicle manufacturers existed in 1900 and that internal combustion–powered vehicles were outnumbered both by steam- and electric-powered vehicles at that time. In any event, experimentation was rampant, and the automobile industry experienced rapid growth (and frequent failure) over its first several decades.

By the end of World War II, the US automobile market was dominated by the "Big Three"—General Motors, Ford, and Chrysler—and consumers had basically settled on internal combustion engines (ICE) to power their vehicles. The extent of this domination is suggested by the fact that the Big Three sold 94.5 percent (!) of the automobiles in America in 1955. Whether it was Dinah Shore singing "See the USA in Your Chevrolet" or Groucho Marx hawking De Sotos on *You Bet Your Life*, the American automobile industry represented the vitality of postwar America, and Americans loved their automobiles.

Unfortunately, the good times came to an end in the 1970s as a result of environmental and safety concerns, OPEC, increasing insurance rates, and global competition. Many enthusiasts view the period from the mid-1970s through the 1980s as the nadir of the American automobile. Inefficient, poorly built, and downright unattractive, these overpriced, underpowered vehicles don't generate much enthusiasm among car lovers.

As an example, the 1976 Cadillac Eldorado was nearly nineteen feet long and weighed over 5,200 pounds. It was powered by a five hundred (!) cubic-inch V-8 that developed only 190 horsepower and drank gasoline to the tune of less than ten miles per gallon. Ah, the good old days! (By comparison, a new Cadillac XTS weighs only 4,200 pounds, is two feet shorter than the '76, generates 410 horsepower, and gets twenty-three miles per gallon!)

Today the consumer again has a choice of motive power: internal combustion, electricity, ICE/electric hybrid, LPG, biodiesel, and, on the horizon, hydrogen fuel cells. Automobile quality, both foreign and domestic, is at an all-time high. Fuel efficiency standards require average miles-per-gallon numbers to increase from 32 mpg to 44 mpg in the not-too-distant future. And the number of automakers has also (re)proliferated, with dozens of manufacturers across the world. We can buy cars produced by firms headquartered in the United States, Japan, Germany, India, Italy, South Korea, the United Kingdom, and China, among others. (China alone boasts over eighty domestic automobile manufacturing firms!)

Additionally, we have seen dramatic developments in transportation technology. Current driver-assist systems keep us from following too closely, warn us when we drift out of our lane, and let us parallel park without even touching the steering wheel! Going one step farther, autonomous vehicles (AVs) appear to be on the horizon. General Motors' Cruise autonomous vehicle unit is valued at nearly fifteen billion dollars, and Kettering University suggests that it is "at the forefront of both the theory and the application of self-driving

See the USA in Your Chevrolet.

Groucho—Seasons Greetings from De Soto.

1976 Cadillac Eldorado.

Kettering University View of Autonomous Vehicles.

vehicles." Meanwhile, Ford's Smart Mobility plan is to have self-driving vehicles on the road by 2021.

Virtually every major automaker appears to be making herculean efforts to develop electric vehicles to challenge Tesla Motors. Audi has rolled out its e-tron line of fully electric vehicles, BMW has launched the i3, and Ford has partnered with Rivian to create an all-electric line of trucks and SUVs.

The rise of ride-sharing apps and firms , like Lyft and Uber in the US, Didi in China, and Grab in Southeast Asia, threatens

Rivian Electric Pickup Truck.

automobile manufacturers with the specter of "peak auto"—a long-term decline in vehicle ownership as consumers increasingly forgo personal automobile ownership for ride-sharing to meet their transportation needs.

St. Louis's Automotive Journey [1]

From a financial viewpoint, the automobile business, in its combined assembling and distributing phases, exceeds any other business activity in St. Louis.

—Thomas, Lewis F. *The Localization of Business Activities in Metropolitan St. Louis*, 1927

St. Louis's location on a major river in the geographic center of the continental US made it ideal for firms hoping to manufacture and sell products across the country. This advantage did not go unnoticed by those in the fledgling automobile industry, and a 1917 St. Louis Chamber of Commerce publication proclaimed:

The geographical location of St. Louis makes it a logical distributing point for automobiles for the West, Southwest, South, Central East and North . . . Freight costs per automobile are lower to these districts than on shipments from Detroit, Cleveland or Indianapolis and the time of delivery is much shorter. The saving in freight is sufficient to give to the dealer practically an increased profit of five per cent.

—(McConnell, p. 205)

By the end of the nineteenth century, St. Louis was the fourth-largest city in the country and poised to take a key role in the fledgling automobile industry.

In 1948, the *St. Louis Globe-Democrat* ran a series entitled "What Makes St. Louis Great?" The article noted that St. Louis had been "a great wagon-building center which supplied the whole southwest" and was second only to Detroit in the volume of automobile production. And in 1955 the *St. Louis Post-Dispatch* proclaimed Missouri the second-ranking automobile producer in the nation, with over 523,000 vehicles produced in the state the previous year. A little over a decade later, *St. Louis Commerce Magazine* proudly proclaimed, "St. Louis is No. 2" in auto manufacturing, second only to Detroit. St. Louis was home to manufacturing plants for each of "the Big Three," annual production exceeded 700,000 vehicles in 1965, and over 16,000 people were employed in automobile manufacturing.

Unfortunately, auto building in St. Louis followed the national trend of postwar boom and then decline. First Ford, then Chrysler, exited auto manufacturing in St. Louis. Chevrolet continues to build vehicles in Wentzville, but the Corvette has gone. As a result of industry changes, St. Louis is no longer second to Detroit in domestic automobile manufacturing. A recent article lists the top five automobile-producing states as Michigan, Ohio, Indiana, Texas, and Illinois. Missouri appears on the list at number seven.

What's Next for St. Louis?

What will St. Louis's role be in the automobile industry going forward? The good news is that civic leaders recognize the continuing importance of automobile-related jobs for the Missouri economy. Former Missouri governor Jay Nixon created the Automotive Jobs Task Force, which recommended increased investment incentives for auto manufacturers and suppliers. St. Louis remains an ideal manufacturing location, with rivers, railroads, airports, and a large labor pool.

There is evidence that efforts to generate a rebound in automobile-related employment are working. According to the Missouri Department of Economic Development, auto manufacturing jobs in Missouri peaked at over 20,800 in 1996 and fell to approximately 5,000 by 2010. However, that number had grown to nearly 14,000 by 2015. Perhaps even more important, organizations like the Missouri Department of Economic Development and the St. Louis Regional Advanced

---

1 This section draws on "St. Louis and the Automobile" by Thomas Eyssell, in *Hidden Assets: Connecting the Past to the Future of St. Louis*, Richard Rosenfeld, ed. Missouri History Museum, St. Louis Press, 2006.

Manufacturing Partnership (RAMP) promote manufacturing activity throughout the state and across the St. Louis region. And according to state statistics, while Missouri is no longer the second-largest producer of vehicles in the US, it is home to dozens of automotive suppliers.

The regional economy continues to grow and evolve. Large firms come and go, while small firms and startups are facilitated through organizations such as the Cambridge Innovation Center, T-REX, CORTEX, and the Danforth Plant Science Center.

The most likely outcome is that the St. Louis region will continue to be a hub for economic development in the region, in both current industries and those yet to be created. Much has changed throughout the decades, but the economic future of the region will undoubtedly look much like the past.

Three Gardner Motor Car Co. and one Moon Motor Car Co. mascots from the collection of John Lowell.

Preserving Vehicles for Future Generations

Websters.com provides the following synonyms for "collector": connoisseur, fancier, hobbyist, authority.

Collectors often display a passion for the things they collect. They seek to learn all they can about both the provenance and the history of these items, their usage in the past, and their link to modern counterparts. Perhaps most importantly, collectors seek out and preserve the objects of their passion, hold them for safekeeping and display, and ultimately pass them along to future generations to enjoy.

The Gateway City's creation, support, and love of the automobile has resulted in the creation and preservation of several notable private and public road vehicle collections over the years. As museums and historical societies began collecting and preserving automobiles just a half-century after they began hitting America's roads, so, too, did private individuals, including those with family ties to the automotive manufacturing history of St. Louis. At almost the same time—near and during World War II—some of the earliest car clubs were founded in St. Louis, including the Horseless Carriage Club of Missouri, which has helped interpret Automobile Row on Locust Street and holds a number of events, shows, and educational programs yearly. It partnered with longtime member Ben Hilliker of Hilliker Corporation in St. Louis in creating and installing bronze interpretive plaques on many historic buildings along Locust Street's Automobile Row. Research and photography performed along that street for this book made clear the positive and marked impact of recognizing those buildings' role in the city's automotive heritage for the street's business owners, residents,

and visitors. Mr. Hilliker has also been the owner and caregiver of several classic vehicles built in St. Louis.

Below we highlight some of St. Louis's most important automobile collections, public and private.

Both George and Andy Dorris, grandsons of St. Louis Motor Carriage Company and Dorris Motor Car Company founder George Preston Dorris, have built personal collections of vehicles built by both their grandfather's automotive makes. As neither believes collector cars should be "trailer queens," both brothers have restored vehicles to operating condition and often drive, rather than trailer, them to events.

George Dorris and John French

Charles P. Gallagher's automobile collection contains automobiles with as few as two cylinders to as many as sixteen. A gorgeous 1942 Lincoln Continental shares Mr. Gallagher's space with a vintage Packard 160, a 1937 Cadillac, and a 1966 Pontiac Bonneville (among others) in two recently refurbished units on St. Louis' historical Produce Row. Mr. Gallagher's automotive tastes are far-ranging, and his site serves as an event space as well as a museum. Mr. Gallagher envisions a new kind of occupant on Produce Row: Car Condominiums retrofitted in vacant units. These solidly built concrete structures boast high ceilings, partial mezzanines, loading docks, 24/7 security, and are centrally located close to both downtown and the Central West End.

Charles P. Gallagher

One of the most notable car collections in St. Louis was assembled by architect Fred Guyton Jr. As a former Army helicopter pilot and co-creator of noted architectural firm Peckham, Guyton, Albers, and Viets Inc., Guyton's broad perspective, appreciation of design, and knowledge of history led him to create a collection of over sixty of the most noted vehicles of the Veteran, Brass, and Classic eras, including several noted Duesenbergs. The collection, noted as one of the world's most significant collections of American pre-war classics, was auctioned in May 2019 following Mr. Guyton's death and generated $11.7 million in sales.

Lee Hunter has been described as an "[i]nventor, industrialist, founder of Hunter Engineering Company and connoisseur of great automobiles." Whether designing automobiles for himself or acquiring classics for his collection, Mr. Hunter displayed a thirst for knowledge and a willingness to share it with other automobile buffs. The Hunter Classic Collection continues to grow in size and quality today under the expert eye of Stephen Brauer, Chairman and CEO of the Hunter Engineering Company, former US ambassador to Belgium, and part-owner of the St. Louis Cardinals.

Mark Hyman founded Hyman Ltd. Classic Cars as the zenith of a lifelong passion for classic automobiles. From the time he was a child, Mark surrounded himself with cars—his passion is a logical extension of his father's business, Easton Tire. As a boy, Mark accompanied his dad on trips to Produce Row to call on truck owners, where he learned the art of schmoozing first hand and cultivated his love of all things motorized. As a teenager, he became involved in the local classic car scene, restoring a 1920 Hudson Doctor's Coupe with his dad along the way. In his mid-twenties, Mark started to realize his passion for classic cars could be turned into a serious business. He sold his first classic, a French Facel Vega project for a profit, which led to another car, and so on, and Hyman Ltd. Classic Cars was born. All along, Mark knew that St. Louis was the only place to base his business, and now, after

more than thirty years, St. Louis has become a hub for many of the world's finest historic cars. Mark and his team have assembled many significant car collections for their clients, several of whom are based in St. Louis. The city's location makes it a logical center for selling cars all over the country and around the world. While Hyman Ltd. is decidedly international in scope, their passion for both the automobile and their hometown ensures the vibrant enthusiast scene right here in St. Louis will be going strong for years to come.

Undoubtedly one of the finest automotive collections in the region is that assembled by Doug Kirberg. Housed in a beautifully renovated warehouse, highlights of Mr. Kirberg's collection are a 1904 Thomas Flyer, a 1954 Cadillac Eldorado built for the Motorama, and a massive 1913 Peerless. Mr. Kirberg's meticulously restored vehicles are not just museum pieces; he has participated in numerous touring events, which he describes as "a great way to see the country at 45 miles per hour." In addition, his "Car Barn" includes numerous bits of rare automobilia—porcelain signs, antique gasoline pumps, and rare oil cans. "Doug's Car Barn" also serves as a venue for charitable events and meetings throughout the year. As with so many collectors, Mr. Kirberg's interest stems from fond childhood memories, and he is generous in sharing his collection with others.

It has been said that great innovations are born when someone recognizes an unfulfilled need and figures out how to fulfill it. In 1970, Robert Pass recognized the need for enclosed transportation of classic and vintage automobiles. Starting with Tom Barrett (of Barrett-Jackson fame) as his first client, Mr. Pass developed the first successful enclosed transport system and built Passport Transport, a firm which revolutionized the vintage automobile hobby by providing safe, secure transportation for vehicles. Passport's fleet exceeded 70 trailers at its peak; the firm was sold to Federal Express in 2000.

Also a noted collector and active participant in the classic car hobby, Mr. Pass has owned several fine pre- and postwar vehicles and celebrity cars (including the one seen on the classic "Giant" movie poster). He has been involved in vintage racing and is a past board president of the world famous Auburn Cord Duesenberg museum in Auburn, Indiana.

Greg R. Rhomberg has assembled what is undoubtedly one of the region's most wide-ranging and eclectic collections of iconic St. Louis memorabilia at his Antique Warehouse. In addition to vintage automobiles, his collection includes neon signs, fire trucks, carnival rides, antique advertising, cash registers, coin-operated devices of every description, and hundreds of other pieces of St. Louis history, large and small. Mr. Rhomberg has been extremely active in the local historical community, serving as co-manager of the Museum of Transportation, as a trustee and collections committee member of the Missouri Historical Society, a board member of the National Building Arts Foundation, and an active member of many local car clubs.

Robert Pass

Greg R. Rhomberg

John Sherman

The "Dean of St. Louis Dealer History" is undoubtedly John Sherman. Mr. Sherman has built an impressive collection of dealership memorabilia: photos, business cards, keychains, advertising literature, license plate advertising, and literally hundreds of related items complement his vast knowledge of local auto dealership history. With over forty years as a professional in the vintage and collector car industry in St. Louis, Mr. Sherman is a wealth of knowledge.

The automobile hobby lives on in the members of the numerous car clubs in St. Louis, as well as in the museums and in the dealers in antique and vintage vehicles spread across the St. Louis region.

Car Clubs

The St. Louis region boasts well over fifty car clubs. Auto enthusiasts join car clubs for a number of reasons, but most clubs exist for similar reasons. Car collectors are educators, volunteers, and benefactors. The members are generous with their time and resources in promoting worthy causes. These causes may be public or private, large or small. Local car clubs have taken it upon themselves to establish educational scholarships, pay medical expenses for a sick member, and sort mountains of car parts, manuals and automobile literature to prepare them for auction to benefit a recently departed club member's heirs. They do all of this while attending car shows, picnics, touring, cruise nights, and monthly dinners. Lifelong friendships are made over the love of the automobile.

While it is not possible to list all of the active car clubs in the region, we provide a representative sampling of clubs that are regional chapters of national organizations and that celebrate our early automotive history.

Horseless Carriage Club of Missouri, http://www.hccmo.com

Classic Car Club of America—Spirit of St. Louis Region,
   https://www.spiritccca.com

Model A Restorers Club—Missouri Valley Region,
   http://www.modelaclub.org

Model T Ford Club of Greater St. Louis,
   http://www.stlmodeltclub.org

Early Ford V8 Club—St. Louis Regional Group,
   https://www.stlv8club.org

Cadillac and LaSalle Club—St. Louis Region,
   https://www.cadillaclasalleclubstl.org

Packard Club—Mississippi Valley, https://www.mvphelm.club

Gateway Fire Historical Society, https://www.facebook.com/Gatewayfire1

Antique Truck Historical Society—Gateway Chapter, https://www.aths.org

Military Vehicle Preservation Assn.—Mid America,
   http://www.mid-americamvpa.org

Dealers in Classic and Vintage Automobiles

Founded by David and Laura Williams in 1994, Fast Lane Classic Cars is a car enthusiast's vision of paradise. A visit to their large and ever-changing inventory of muscle cars, hot rods, motorcycles, collector cars, trucks, and vintage signage testifies to St. Louis's undying love for the road. https://www.fastlanecars.com

With an inventory of vehicles that often numbers in the thousands and crosses over a century in age, Gateway Classic Cars features vehicles worthy of everything from a Sunday afternoon drive to setting record times at the local track. https://www.gatewayclassiccars.com

Charles Schmitt has been in the "Thoroughbred Car Business" for over fifty years. At one time Charles Schmitt and Company was the largest seller of Rolls Royces in the United States, and Mr. Schmitt counted among his customers some of the most recognized celebrities of the day. Located on Kingshighway, this firm remains a link to the past and to really fine automobiles, foreign and domestic, for the discriminating buyer. https://www.schmittmotorcars.com

The "Collector Car Gallery" of Daniel Schmitt and Company provides another source of exotic and classic vehicles for the collector. Whether one's tastes run to a Model A or an Aston Martin, this dealer may have it somewhere on his four-acre dealership.

https://www.schmitt.com

Museums

Founded just after the Civil War, the Missouri Historical Society develops, preserves, and interprets a collection of over 175,000 artifacts for nearly a half-million visitors each year. If it happened or came from St. Louis and you have questions or want to learn more about it, you'll likely find the answers in either the Missouri History Museum on Lindell Boulevard or the Library and Research Center on Skinker Boulevard. https://www.mohistory.org

The Moto Museum caters to the motorcycle enthusiast. With a collection of foreign and domestic motorcycles extending back to the turn of the twentieth century, the rider or collector is sure to find something to his/her taste. The museum is open to the public and free (!), and also serves as a venue for special events. https://www.themotomuseum.com

Joe Scott III (left) stands with Joe Scott II, who is wearing an award medal for Best in Show: 1937 Packard Super 8 Coupe Roadster at the 2018 Fort Lauderdale Yacht Club Concours D'Elegance.

Dave Mungenast Sr. didn't just sell vehicles. He loved them. This collection began with Dave's personal collection of automobiles and motorcycles and has developed to include multiple generations of the best road vehicles built in places ranging from St. Louis to the other side of the world. The Mungenast Classic Automobiles and Motorcycles Museum is located at 5625 and 5626 Gravois Avenue and includes both an event space and restaurant. http://www.mungenastclassicmuseum.com

The world-renowned vehicle collection of the National Museum of Transportation began with the saving of an historic mule-drawn streetcar from the scrap drives in World War II and has grown to become one of the largest and most significant collections of North American transportation vehicles, ranging from one of the oldest surviving automobiles built in St. Louis to the largest successful railroad steam locomotive ever built. https://www.transportmuseumassociation.org

The St. Louis Car Museum recently celebrated its twenty-fifth anniversary. The former Bowl-o-Rama building was converted to a museum and sales operation by Joe Scott II. The St. Louis Car Museum encompasses over 85,000 square feet of indoor space filled with everything from classic cars to vintage motorcycles to automobilia of virtually every type. The Car Museum is open to the public, and for a small admission fee, one can spend an afternoon (or a day!) wandering among the roughly 150 vintage cars, toys, gas pumps, and other automobilia. https://www.stlouiscarmuseum.com

Car Shows

While impossible to list all the car events around St. Louis, these perennial car shows deserve honorable mention.

The Easter Concours d'Elegance held by the Horseless Carriage Club of Missouri in Forest Park kicks off the annual show season with vehicles conserved or restored to the highest standards.

The National Museum of Transportation hosts a regular series of themed shows throughout the season ranging from early horseless carriages to modern fire trucks. Admission to the shows is free, and discounts to the remainder of the museum and its memberships are frequently offered.

Car clubs throughout the St. Louis area hold their own shows in a variety of settings ranging from vintage restaurants to race tracks to churches, and it's hard to find a weekend between Easter and Halloween on which multiple car shows aren't being held within fifty miles of downtown St. Louis.

JET
DINER
SHELL
TEXACO
FINA
Mobil
2416115
IC5C
GREASE
ROTARY LIFT
ROTARY LIFT

This circa 1915 view of Twelfth Street evidences a time when horse-drawn vehicles, streetcars, and horseless carriages shared the streets of St. Louis. Courtesy Missouri History Museum, St. Louis.

INDEX

A pedestrian at Eighteenth and Locust stops for a Ford Model T—likely built in St. Louis—and its passengers in 1918. Even with the upper front glass folded, the young lady and gentlemen in the car managed to keep their hats. Courtesy Missouri History Museum, St. Louis.

I

J

Men and automobile tire repair truck outside the H. Bender Firestone Tire dealership at 4388 Olive Street in 1906. By 1908, the City of St. Louis had issued 1,900 automobile licenses. Courtesy Missouri History Museum, St. Louis.

K

K-cars, 159
Kahn, Albert, 67
Kansas, 16, 85
Kansas City, 16, 85
Kardell Motor Company, 123
Kentucky, 4, 152, 154
Kettering University, 164–165
King Dodge, 131
Kirberg, Doug, 172
Kirkwood, James P., 6
Kissel Company, 36
Koehler, 31
Koochook Rubber Company, 124
Kraft, J. F., 14, 16
Krenning, Harry B., 41–42

L

Laclede Avenue, 36, 60, 88
Laclede Building, 11
Laclede's Landing, 56
Lakedel Automobile Company, 37
Lampsteed Kampkar, 40
Langan, Louis, 17
Lasker Motor Company, 87, 92
Leach, Brouster, and Company, 116
League of American Wheelmen, 9–10
Leeper Automobile Company, 64
Leeper, Jesse, 64
Leeper, Stewart, 64
Lemon Automobile and Manufacturing Company, 30
Lemp, Charles, 77
Lewis, J. D. Perry, 16
Lewis, Meriwether, 3
Liguest, Pierre Laclède, 3
Lindbergh, Charles, 66, 113
Lindell Boulevard, 13, 20, 30, 175
Livingston, James, xv, 29
Lockheed, 70
Locomobile Company of Missouri, 115
Locust Street, 96–129
    See also 11, 16–17, 22, 58, 63, 85–86, 130–131, 134, 169, 182
Logan Motor Dispatch, 58
Louisiana Purchase Exposition, 11
Louisville, 4
Lucas Place, 16
Luedinghaus & Espenschied Wagon Company, 81
Luedinghaus Truck, 79–80
Lurie Motor Car Company, 108
Lycoming, 69
Lyft, 165

M

MacDonald, Stewart, 33
Macintosh Automobile Company, 67

N

A curved dash holds a premier position in Oldsmobile's exhibit in the Palace of Transportation at the 1904 World's Fair. Courtesy Missouri History Museum, St. Louis.

View of Charles J. Knight and passengers in Stearns car; F.B. Stearns Company building in background. Stamped on back: "Photographic illustration by Nick Lazarnick, 230 Park Ave., N.Y." Handwritten on back: "Biography--Knight, Charles J. Knight at wheel of Stearns (Cleveland); inventor of Knight sleeve-valve motor, first adopted by English Daimler after others adopted it in Europe, was bought by John N. Willys by Willys Knight, overland car at Toledo." Courtesy Detroit Public Library.